Postcards from the Cinema is the book Serge Daney, one of the greatest of film critics, never wrote. It is based around an interview that was to be the starting point for a book, a project cut short by Daney's death. *Postcards* turns a history of cinema into a profound meditation on the art and politics of film.

Daney's passionate and lucid engagement with film, combined with his concern for journalistic clarity, effectively created film criticism as a genre. Equally at home with the theories of Deleuze, Lacan and Debord as he was with the movie-making of Bunuel, Godard and Ray, Daney was also a fan of Jerry Lewis and Hitchcock. At the same time—and before his time—championed the critical analysis of television and other audio-visual media.

Long-awaited, this is the first book-length translation of Daney's work, testimony to a life lived with a fierce love of film.

SERG DANEY was a writer and eventually editor-in-chief for the highly influential film journal *Cahiers du cinéma*. He went on to write for the newspaper *Liberation*, and founded the film journal *Trafic*.

Postcards from the Cinema

Postcards from the Cinema

SERGE DANEY

Translated by Paul Douglas Grant

Oxford • New York

This work is published with the support of the French Ministry of Culture – Centre National du Livre

This book is supported by the French Ministry of Foreign Affairs as part of the Burgess programme run by the Cultural Department of the French Embassy in London (www.frenchbooknews.com)

First published in France, 1994, by P.O.L.

This English translation first published in 2007 by
Berg
Editorial offices:
First Floor, Angel Court, 81 St Clements Street, Oxford OX4 1AW, UK
175 Fifth Avenue, New York, NY 10010, USA

Berg is the imprint of Oxford International Publishers Ltd.

Library of Congress Cataloging-in-Publication Data
Daney, Serge.
[Persévérance. English]
Postcards from the cinema / Serge Daney ; translated by Paul Douglas Grant.
p. cm.
Includes bibliographical references and index.
ISBN-13: 978-1-84520-650-5 (cloth)
ISBN-10: 1-84520-650-9 (cloth)
ISBN-13: 978-1-84520-651-2 (pbk.)
ISBN-10: 1-84520-651-7 (pbk.)
1. Motion pictures. 2. Daney, Serge. 3. Film critics—France—Interviews. I. Title.
PN1995.D3213 2007
791.43—dc22 2006029772

British Library Cataloguing-in-Publication Data
A catalogue record for this book is available from the British Library.

ISBN-13 978 1 84520 650 5 (Cloth)
978 1 84520 651 2 (Paper)
ISBN-10 1 84520 650 9 (Cloth)
1 84520 651 7 (Paper)

Typeset by Avocet Typeset, Chilton, Aylesbury, Bucks
Printed in the United Kingdom by Biddles Ltd, King's Lynn.

www.bergpublishers.com

Contents

To Huguette Daney

Introduction: The History of an Absence

> [E]very image of the past that is not recognized by the present as one of its concerns threatens to disappear irretrievably.
>
> Walter Benjamin

The work of French film critic Serge Daney has for too long remained a gap in the world of English-language film criticism. In fact, his proper introduction is so overdue that the very mention of this deficiency is itself becoming something of a cliché. Apart from a few texts that have shown up on the internet or in various collections, there has been no English translation of a book by Serge Daney. Obviously lacunae, fissures, and slight treatment will always haunt the substance of our knowledge and our corpus of world art and literature. From France alone we are still on unfamiliar terrain with Jean-Louis Schefer's writing on cinema, while Jean-Claude Biette remains an obscure figure both as a filmmaker and as a critic; Philippe Arnaud, Nicole Brenez, Alain Philippon, Alain Bergala ... a seemingly endless "missing" or "most wanted" list. But it is an easy and even futile task to simply point out what is lacking. To fill the various gaps it's not enough to merely cite the absence and give it a proper name; the work of reparation must be undertaken as well. With this end in mind, a number of events have been produced to try to bring Serge Daney to the English-speaking world.

In the fall of 2002, Block Cinema in Chicago hosted *Serge Daney: 10 Years After*, a lecture and screening series in which the films that held a primary place in Daney's criticism, those he cited, admired, and *lived*, were shown. The Harvard Film Archive in Cambridge, Massachusetts followed suit in January 2004 with *Beyond Film Criticism: A Symposium in Homage to Serge Daney*, a day of lectures given by an international cast of critics discussing the work of Daney as well as the task and state of film criticism in general. However, a familiar problem reared its head at the event: the portion of the symposium specifically addressing the work and person of Daney was primarily the office of the French-speaking guests, while the rest of the panel remained somewhat in the dark. How could it be otherwise, as it's obviously an extremely difficult task to introduce the work of a writer whose work is barely translated and whose name has remained little more than a footnote in the English-speaking world of film studies. To confuse matters, on those rare occasions when Daney is referenced, something still gets in the way of proper translation, as in Trihn T Mihn Ha's book *Cinema Interval*, where he is referred to in the index as *Sergei* Daney, and in John Kreidl's Book *Jean-Luc Godard*, where he is again in the index, this time as Serge *Dany*.

At this stage of the English-language encounter with Daney, there is one document that best characterizes the need for his words in English, and that is film critic Jonathan Rosenbaum's inspired letter to the editors of *Trafic*. "Daney en anglais: lettre à Trafic" was published in the spring 2001 issue entitled *Serge Daney: après, avec*, a special ten-year anniversary issue of the journal that Daney founded shortly before his death. It also appeared in English on the *senses of cinema* website. In the letter Rosenbaum begins by describing the importance of Daney in French film criticism and then turns, with some cynicism, towards the issue of Daney's strange absence in English. Although Rosenbaum cites attempts to smuggle Daney into English through various back doors, he remarks that his work is situated on a strange border: on the one hand, Daney is a popular writer, and perhaps too popular to interest an academic readership and press; on the other, his writing may not be sufficiently popular. A quick glance at just about any Daney text will reveal an erudite thinker whose complexity can rival that of just about any post-structuralist writer. The problem then is that the work might be considered by publishers to be too academic for the mainstream.

If Rosenbaum's suggestion is correct, it could account for the next to non-existent translation, citation, and study of Daney's work in English, but the issue is further aggravated by a dearth of secondary literature in French. This is particularly suspicious given the high regard for Daney in France, where he is considered by many to be the greatest French film critic since André Bazin. He is often praised as the guru of cinephilia, and it is not uncommon to hear comparisons of his work with that of the great Roland Barthes. Gilles Deleuze wrote a letter to Daney that placed the critic in the lineage of André Bazin as well as the nineteenth-century Austrian art historian Alois Riegl. Jean-Luc Godard—one of Serge Daney's most longstanding interlocutors, who consecrated a chapter in his monumental *Histoire(s) du Cinéma* to an interview with Daney—remarked in an interview with Youssef Ishaghpour that criticism as he understood it disappeared when Daney died, and he spoke of a critical-literary tradition that moves from Diderot, to Baudelaire, to Daney. Again, with such prestigious lip service, it is a strange phenomenon to find so little written about his work, and the rare pieces of existing literature on Daney that do appear often suffer from a peculiar mimesis: the secondary texts end up repeating the form of Daney's texts themselves, that is, they are generally short prescient articles or personal accounts. The clearest examples of such literature are the two posthumously published special editions of *Trafic* and *Cahiers du cinéma* dedicated to Daney, in which a number of intellectuals, co-workers, filmmakers, and critics contribute short essays describing Daney, his writing, and his impact. The essays amount to non-systematic studies of aspects of Daney's work and life, and most of the writers attempt to define Daney for themselves, through accounts of personal friendship or critical affinities, that is to say, they are ultimately autobiographical pieces. As interesting, and often moving, as these pieces are, they unfortunately don't amount to objective, critical, or productive studies of Daney's work.

In March 2005 Les Éditions Montparnasse released a DVD version of *Itineraire d'un cinéfils*, a three-hour filmed interview between Serge Daney and Régis Debray. To celebrate the release the movie theater Reflets-Medicis in Paris hosted *Le Festival Serge Daney*. Like its American counterparts, the festival showed the foundational films over the course of a week and then each night presented a debate with a number of Daney's contemporaries or "heirs." The result: minor turnout and major cancellations at almost every screening. Once again this stubborn aporia persisted. Serge Toubiana and Jean Douchet stood before the meager audience and admitted their own difficulty in talking about Daney and his work—which is to say even those who would seem to be the most capable of speaking eloquently and effusively on the subject were also admitting a kind of defeat. Should we consider this melancholic stammering as the only possible reflection on the work of a self-proclaimed melancholic critic? Or should we instead suggest that the resistance to summary in Daney is not due to a fault with his writing, but is in fact a result of the complexity and singularity of his thinking?

Daney's first published piece of critical writing was *Un Art Adulte*, an essay on Howard Hawks' *Rio Bravo*, which appeared in an issue of *Visages du cinéma* in 1962. *Visages du cinéma* was a short-lived magazine (two issues were published in total) produced by Daney and his friend Louis Skorecki. Daney began writing for *Cahiers* in 1964 at the end of the famous "yellow period"—the name refers to the yellow cover of *Cahiers* that reigned until 1964. The mythic and weighty early days of *Cahiers* had gathered around its illustrious tables the famous "Young Turks": Eric Rohmer, François Truffaut, Jacques Rivette, Jean-Luc Godard, and Claude Chabrol, a group of young cinephiles that nourished, if not gorged, itself on cinema. Under the guidance of André Bazin these writers took seriously films that were thus far overlooked. They found merit in American B-movies and in particular championed Lang, Hitchcock, and Hawks: thus the moniker *Hitchcocko-Hawksiens*. They concentrated on *mise-en-scène* and spoke of the *politiques des auteurs*. By 1959 these critics moved behind the camera and revolutionized cinema: the *Nouvelle Vague* (New Wave) was born. Daney's participation at *Cahiers* thus began at the height of the New Wave and his stay extended through the structuralist and Maoist periods, until ultimately he and Serge Toubiana took over as editors in chief.

The mid-1960s was a period in which *Cahiers*' writing on film would take on the language of structuralism, semiotics, and psychoanalysis. The magazine began to demand of its readership a knowledge that the previous cinephilic drafts didn't require. Barthes' influence on criticism found its way into the journal's writing; Althusser and Lacan became the guiding theoretical lights. In this period, *Cahiers*' writing was difficult but remained readable; these were incredibly fecund years whose influence on film theory is still clearly felt today. What followed was the Maoist period of the early

1970s, a turbulent time when *Cahiers* suffered the loss of financial support and a major decrease in readership. The militant Marxist-Leninist perspective distanced *Cahiers* from many of its original adherents and film began to disappear as the primary object of the magazine. If *Cahiers* had been trying for some time to separate itself from its past, this new mode of criticism was a successful, if violent, break with its former idealism, which is to say it was a break with Bazin. One of the most telling gestures of this period was the editorial decision to stop putting images on the cover, as well as almost entirely eradicating the images inside the magazine as well. There were scissions, divisions, and mock trials of members of the editorial team who weren't writing in accordance with the "party line." The period is often dismissed as a kind of going astray: for example, Antoine DeBaecque in his impressive history of *Cahiers du cinéma* moves through these years, giving them a factual, and even unceremonious, treatment, suggesting that each blunder was just further proof of having abandoned the "good" cinephilic object. However, although politically we can see the mistakes, the straying, and the posturing, it would be wise to avoid jumping on the easy bandwagon of righteous hindsight and look instead at the political and cultural climate of the time, especially in France. A post-'68 politics had to account for the failure of the *événements*, and by extension the failure of cinema and culture, both with a capital C. We can read the fierce criticism from this period, composed with a brio rarely surpassed, as a kind of fidelity to a radical but badly injured cinematic project. In the gnashing of theoretical teeth one can make out the faint traces of a nascent mourning. The critics were placing what they loved on the chopping block precisely to save it. It is a great melancholic *démarche*: if the choices are between loss and forfeiture, it is better to cut away, to cut up, and to cannibalize what one loves, rather than merely ceding it to the "winning" side. Ultimately, the adage of the baby and the bathwater might here be put to good use.

When Daney and Toubiana took over as editors in chief, they co-authored the essay "*Cahiers* Today" for the May 1974 issue, which announced a break with *Cahiers*' Maoist past and in a sense inaugurated a kind of return to cinephilia. Daney remained at *Cahiers* until 1981, at which time he left to write for *Libération*, the left-wing daily newspaper created in 1973 by, among others, Jean-Paul Sartre and Serge July. At *Libération* Daney expanded both his production, since he was writing on a daily basis, and his scope. He began to extend his focus from criticism of films in the movie theater to films shown on television, and then even further to news broadcasts, commercials, and tennis. He also started the section *Rebonds*, opinion pages with frequent contributions from well-known French intellectuals, which continues to exist today. Finally, Daney's last great migration was leaving *Libération* in 1991 to create, with a few others, the film journal *Trafic*. This was a move away from the daily production of *Libération* to a quarterly publication that would permit more sustained criticism and lengthy literary meditations on the current state and future of cinema.

Over the course of his career Daney published a number of books, all of which were collections of essays and articles that he had written for *Cahiers du cinéma*, *Libération*, and other diverse reviews, but ultimately no complete book, or, as Toubiana remarks in the Preface in citing Daney, no "real" book. However this account needs to be modified in light of a 1973 publication entitled *Procès à: Baby Doc (Duvalier, père & fils)*, a book on Haitian politics by one Raymond Sapène. Raymond Sapène is in fact Serge Daney, but apparently this work did not in his mind complete the requirements of a "real" book. Since his death from AIDS in 1992 there have been more collections published and two books that resemble something close to a "real" book, yet they still did not fulfill the demands of such a work. *L'exercice a été profitable Monsieur* (the title in English would be *The Exercise was Beneficial, Sir* and is a quote from Fritz Lang's *Moonfleet*, one of the foundational films for Daney) is a journal taken from Daney's computer, and it is a phenomenal book that gives the reader an insight into Daney's thought processes. *L'exercice* actually contains rare attempts to define certain recurring terms, but is ultimately a kind of *Grundrisse* that was not intended to be published. Then there is *Postcards from the Cinema* (*Persévérance*) (1994), translated in English for the first time, which is Serge Toubiana's effort to complete the task of a real book for Daney. *Postcards from the Cinema,* coming the closest to fulfilling the demand, is composed of a Preface by Toubiana, a previously published essay, "The Tracking Shot in *Kapo*," and the main body of the work, which is an interview with Daney.

By the time *Trafic* was established, Daney was becoming more and more visibly ill from AIDS, and, recognizing that they were soon to lose this enigmatic figure, a number of Daney's friends and admirers gathered around him and tirelessly interviewed him to get his last will and testament "on film" and paper. They wanted to make sure we knew what he was bequeathing the world, this dear friend of cinema, the strangely eternal child who forever made his identification known with John Mohune in *Moonfleet* or John Harper in *Night of the Hunter*, "the most beautiful American film ever made." The documents that result from this period make up a part of Daney's work proper, from the interviews at *Esprit*, to *Itineraire d'un cinéfils*, to what might be considered one of the most original pieces of film criticism: *Postcards*, a book in the form of a "cine-biography."

Returning to the difficulty of summarizing or totalizing that shadows Daney, it can now be seen that he traversed a number of epochs, all which were rife with the intellectual fashions of the day. Though we can read in his work the influence of the various epochs in which he was writing, it is perhaps more interesting to note how he maintains certain conceptual frameworks, but without the concomitant dogmatism that often accompanies such trends. So if developing a "Daneyan" lexicon is difficult, and maybe even a hindrance to the academic exploitation of his work, we can also find in that "stumbling block" the good postmodern utopia: Daney's lack of frozen jargon is precisely what sets him aside from a good number of his contemporaries, and in many respects creates a criticism that is forever dodging a totalizing discourse, yet it is not effete, liberal, or flaccidly centrist. One might think of the whole of Daney's work in terms of Theodor Adorno's *Minima Moralia*: the fragments are the form and the form itself expresses the non-totalizing synthesis. The fragments as form describe an experience, an experience of the twentieth century and its inextricable relationship with the history of cinema, or cinema and its relationship to television. And as radical as it would feel to suggest that the resistance of Daney's work to systematization is the realization of a criticism that the sponge of late capitalism fails to co-opt, it is time to reveal the ace in the hole, to bring out the enticing upside: as of late there are at least three impressive uses of Serge Daney, productive ways that are not mere repetitions of style or content: Censier student Theo Lichtenberger's 2005 thesis *Une traversée de l'univers Daney*; Suzanne Liandrat-Guigues and Jean-Louis Leutrat's *Penser le cinema* (2001), and Alain Bergala's pedagogic use of Daney in *L'Hypothèse cinema* (2002). We can only hope that these formidable documents will one day make their way into English.

The good news for the anglophone reader: this is the beginning of a wonderful encounter with an untapped source of inspiration for ways to think cinema. *Postcards from the Cinema* is an eminently readable book, full of anecdotes, theoretical musings, "Daneyan" analogies between tennis or bullfighting and the cinema, meditations on the Holocaust, freedom, homosexuality, and that strange fascination dressed up as an illness, cinephilia. It is the kind of work that is both satisfying in its own right, while simultaneously inciting a desire to read more, to know more, and let us hope we will see more of Daney's work translated into English in the coming years. The bad news—and here we will have to tarry with our own grief, or perhaps it is merely disappointment: there is a particularly informative, yet grim passage early in *À la recherche du temps perdu* in which Proust describes his experience with *mémoire involontaire*. He suggests that the past resides in objects, and that it is for each of us to find the object that will explode the past, unleash it before us again. The sad truth, he adds, is that there is no guarantee one will find the object. There is thus a modicum of vertigo in imagining the incalculable visions, both ecstatic and horrifying, that the experience of stumbling upon this object could deliver unto us. And then the crushing blow of a sometimes detestable empirical world, the unwieldy python of chronology, of no guarantees, and of chance that announces that in fact it is unlikely that we will have this experience. It is thus with Daney. A flash of hope, someone who has moved through melancholy, very nearly completed the work of mourning and begun the process of writing the disaster with this strange new object *Trafic*, and then the conduit for recounting the new object is snatched away from us. For if, on the one hand, Proust only describes the object, he also creates it by suggesting its possibility: are we not forever locked in some sort of corporeal palindrome where our point of departure is always our point of return? Perhaps Daney pointed to an off-ramp that simply vanished as all horizons do? The heat of the concrete that blurs its future definition. Concrete: what else have we ever really considered to be material?

A Note on the Translation and Acknowledgments

Spending time with this book and the work of Serge Daney in general has been the moving process of getting to know someone, someone who is no longer there to immediately respond but somehow persists in answering questions, posing them, and accompanying. As Daney so often spoke of those he didn't know as friends, companions on the road, whether writers, directors, or characters in a movie, so has he become just such a figure for me. This experience I believe is not the result of merely reading someone, or of getting to know the work, but rather of translating a work. It happened often during the translation process that I would suddenly be quite impressed with myself for the ideas I was formulating, the grand thoughts on history, cinema, or the Holocaust, which is to say I was proud of the book that "I" was writing. What a strange awakening to come back to myself and remember I was just translating.

Though the entire process is one of making choices between this strange equivalence of words, for the most part there is a kind of intuitive sense of which meaning is which, what word corresponds. But there are a few instances that might be up for debate:

Cahiers du cinéma has been left in the original, or as *Cahiers* when appropriate, meaning no article is added. The temptation to write *The Cahiers* was great, but it seems that the tradition of leaving off the article reigned.

Politiques des Auteurs remains in the French. Andrew Sarris's translation as the *Auteur theory* seems to be controversial enough that it is better to let him keep the term while letting the French term stand.

Finally the word "cinema," which in French defines the whole of the idea of cinema, as well as the movie theater. In English, "Cinema," with a capital *C*, or with the article "the," is reserved primarily for academia, and, if I may say, can, in the wrong context, have a slightly pretentious ring to it. The options in English are manifold: film, films, movies, pictures, flicks, etc. Many words, and yet in hearing the tone of Daney it was extremely difficult to translate *cinéma* into movies.

Occasionally he would use the term "film" or "films," which made things easier, but Cinema has for the most part, in my translation, remained Cinema. Though I distrust the mildly elitist ring, something that might be contrary to Daney's avowed populism, I was unprepared to translate this life-affirming object, this life-changing process, in brief, this life, to the word "movies," which simply does not carry the gravitas of the weighty if sometimes pretentious "cinema."

There are many people to thank for their time and assistance: Ronnie Bronstein; Nicole Brenez; Mary Ann Douglas; David Gordon; Andy and Robbie Grant; Jeff Jackson; Reed King; Laurent Kretschmar; Théo Lichtenberger for sharing his own work on Daney; Tristan Palmer at Berg Publishers; Ethan Spigland; Amy Tondu and the French Fulbright Commission; Romy Wettstein; and Sean Williams. Most importantly my thanks go to Pascale Wettstein, without whom it would have been impossible to accomplish the translation; her help made what was sometimes risible legible. *P, c'est surtout pour vous.*

Paul Douglas Grant

Preface to the French Edition

It was the end of December 1991, between Christmas and New Year's Day. A few days before going to Israel for *Cahiers du cinéma Week* I visited an already ill Serge Daney.

As usual our conversation touched on different subjects: current cinema, the state of *Cahiers*, the launching of his journal *Trafic*, and then the state of Serge's health. He spoke of his desire to write a book—in his opinion his last—for which he had already chosen the title: *Persévérance*.[1] It was to be a "real" book, not just a collection of articles.

He told me about his desire to take the material of his life as a cinephile and finally tell his story. He was clear that the book would open with his essay on the tracking shot in *Kapo*, referring to an article by Jacques Rivette in the June 1961 issue of *Cahiers du cinéma* that denounced Gillo Pontecorvo's film.

This article had a considerable impact on the then 17-year-old Serge Daney; it provoked both an aesthetic and moral shock that would determine his fate as a future critic for *Cahiers du cinéma*. Throughout the 1970s and 1980s, we often collectively cited the Rivette article, just like his famous "Letter on Rossellini,"[2] two texts that would contribute to the foundation of the critical edifice of a journal like *Cahiers du cinéma*.

Serge never stopped coming back to this, inscribing his intellectual trajectory in the theoretical filiation of these texts: the concentration camps, the impossibility of cinema to continue telling stories while "forgetting" Hiroshima, the rupture of modern cinema, Rosellini and Godard. This theoretical itinerary remained in part obscure for me; I only had an abstract, and rather fuzzy, understanding of it. I simply trusted Daney in his thought and never really developed an understanding of it. I was missing a link that, later, Serge would reveal to me.

Over the course of this visit at the end of December, just as every other time I stopped by to see him at rue Traversiere, I asked where he was with *Persévérance*. *Trafic* was taking up almost all of his time, as well as what was left of his energy. This is what he held onto the most. The rest of the time he dedicated to seeing his friends. Yet, I saw his sadness, and even his bitterness, at not having enough strength to undertake this book.

The year ended strangely. For some months there had been an uneasiness between us. Serge was upset with me for something—which I will explain in a moment. I later made amends: the silence on the issue was quite heavy. I felt guilty and had to give Serge some proof of my friendship.

As I left him that day, I decided to send him a note as soon as possible proposing we undertake a long recorded interview that could serve as a point of departure for his book. I also suggested we leave Paris for a couple of days to have a bit of peace and quiet.

Upon returning, a note signed S.D. dated January 4, 1992: "Your letter obviously touched me very much. This added to my sadness, the (selfish) suspicion that you weren't 'on my side.' We should have done this book of interviews a year ago. This time it's my fault. As always, I'm scattered and the mess is real. We can try to do this strange project (a 'cine-biography') together. Rather quickly."

A year before, it was in fact my fault. Serge was upset with me for not being on his side during the "Berri Affair." For those who don't know or who have forgotten, Claude Berri had subpoenaed *Libération*, following a particularly inspired article by Serge against his film *Uranus*. Berri obtained a "right to response," which was both weak in content and mediocre in form, and which ended with a vulgar "See you later, princess." It was the first time that a filmmaker obtained, by means of a warrant, the right to respond to a non-defamatory article. Serge was profoundly hurt that this would be published in *Libération*, his journal, without anyone defending him.

He was also upset with his friends, and therefore me, and he was right: I didn't show my solidarity, and I didn't offer him comfort. The climate was strange; it was the middle of the Gulf War.

Eventually we made up, but this episode left its scars. Serge never missed an opportunity to come back to it. It was a stage in his life when he was settling scores, with extreme clarity, without lenience towards himself or others. That's the way it was, and the only demonstration of friendship was to be there.

He had written to me "Rather quickly." In fact, it was an emergency.

At the beginning of February Serge went to Marseilles with Raymond Bellour for a conference on cinema and to publicly present the journal *Trafic*.

We agreed to meet near Aix-en-Provence, at Éguilles, where I had reserved two rooms at the Hotel Belvedere, from Friday the 7th to Sunday the 9th of February.

The interview took place there. Our rooms were adjacent, and I joined Serge in his room for the interview, which lasted as long as possible. In spite of his fatigue, he spoke for hours on end, and his ideas remained clear. He recounted the story of his life, that of a "*cine-fils*" whose cine-biography had come to its end. It was incredibly moving to hear a friend who knew he was close to death speak with such ease and understanding about his own life, his childhood, and his journey, without a word of complaint or injustice.

At Éguilles, I learned things I had never known, things he had never said to anyone. It wasn't a confession, or what might be banally called self-analysis. Rather it was inscribed in a personal, mastered, and logical script. Serge was in the process of serenely arranging the final pieces of a puzzle, that of his life.

I never really understood the importance for Serge of the Rivette article on *Kapo* (a film, moreover, he admitted to having never seen) until that February. Over the course of our long interview, which resulted in this book, he spoke for the first time about his father, this figure who was secret and unknown to him. That day Serge concluded his story, his passage from a child born in 1944—the year of *Rome, Open City* and the discovery of the camps—to the young man who, through the love of cinema, was going to write his life, that is, to merge it with a certain history of cinema. The "tracking shot in *Kapo*," the "Letter on Rosellini," his relationship with *Cahiers du cinéma*, the defense of Straub and Godard articulated around an aesthetic of resistance, the love of foreign languages, the taste for travel, the cult of friendship, the transition to *Libération*, illness, the birth of *Trafic* … Suddenly, the *biographical* inscription echoed a theoretical discourse, giving it its true scope.

The "missing link" finally illuminated Serge's itinerary for me. Though we had been friends for twenty years, having spent many of them in front of each other in the same office of *Cahiers du cinéma*, it wasn't until that day that I truly understood him.

The flight from Marseilles back to Paris was difficult. In the airport he told me it was probably his last trip—he who loved to travel so much.

He wanted to move quickly. I had the tapes transcribed as fast as possible, giving them to Anne-Marie Faux, who worked with intelligence. Then I gave it all to Serge. He promised to rework the first draft. He didn't have enough strength to both man *Trafic* and take on this task of rewriting. During each of my visits, I discreetly asked how it was coming along. "It's coming, it's coming ...." I had my doubts.

One day he told me he had begun a first rewrite on his computer. He didn't have time to finish the work. He died of AIDS on June 12, 1992, five months after our interview at Éguilles.

For a long time I hesitated to publish this manuscript because only the first part of our interview had been entirely reviewed by Serge. For those who know his writing, it's all there: his concision, sense of story and style. As for the second part, I reviewed it myself, trying to be as faithful as possible to his words.

It seemed obvious to me that his article "The Tracking Shot in *Kapo*" should open this book, because it was Serge's intention to make it the first chapter of his book. It is the last text he published in *Trafic*.

Serge Toubiana

Part I

CHAPTER 1

The Tracking Shot in *Kapo*

First published in Trafic, 4, Fall 1992, P.O.L. Éditions

Among the many films I've never seen there is not only *October*, *Le jour se lève*, and *Bambi*, but the obscure *Kapo* as well. A film about the concentration camps shot in 1960 by the leftist Italian Gillo Pontecorvo, *Kapo* was by no means a landmark in the history of cinema. Am I the only one who has never seen this film but has never forgotten it? I haven't seen *Kapo* and yet at the same time I have seen it. I've seen it because someone showed it to me—with words. This movie, whose title—functioning as a kind of password—has accompanied my life of cinema, I know it only through a short text: the review written by Jacques Rivette in the June 1961 issue of *Cahiers du cinéma*. It was the 120th issue and the article was entitled "On Abjection." Rivette was 33 and I was 17. I had probably never uttered the word "abjection" in my life.

Rivette didn't recount the film's narrative in his article. Instead he was content to describe one shot in a single sentence. The sentence, engraved in my memory, read: "Just look at the shot in *Kapo* where Riva commits suicide by throwing herself on electric barbed wire: the man who decides at this moment to track forward and reframe the dead body in a low-angle shot—carefully positioning the raised hand in the corner of the final frame—deserves only the most profound contempt." Therefore a simple camera movement could be the *one* movement not to make. The movement one must—*obviously*—be abject to make. As soon as I read those lines I knew the author was absolutely right.

Abrupt and luminous, Rivette's text allowed me to give voice to this particular form of abjection. My revulsion had found the words to express itself. But there was more. This revolt was accompanied by a feeling both less pure and less clear: a sense of relief in realizing that I had just obtained my first conviction as a future critic. Over the years, "the tracking shot in *Kapo*" would become my portable dogma, the axiom that wasn't up for discussion, the breaking point of any debate. I would definitely have nothing to do or share with anyone who didn't immediately *feel* the abjection of "the tracking shot in *Kapo*."

At the time this type of refusal was common. Looking at the raging and exasperated style of Rivette's article, I sensed that furious debates had already taken place and it already seemed obvious to me that cinema was the echo box of all polemic. The war in Algeria was ending, and because it hadn't been filmed, it brought suspicion to bear upon any representation of history. Everybody seemed to understand that things such as taboo figures, criminal aptitudes, and forbidden cuts existed—especially in cinema. Godard's famous expression that a tracking shot was a "moral affair" was one of those truths that could no longer be questioned. Not by me anyway.

Rivette's article was published in *Cahiers du cinéma*, three years prior to the end of the yellow period. Did I sense that the text couldn't have been published in any other magazine, that it belonged to *Cahiers* just as, later on, I would belong to it? In any case I found my family. Therefore it wasn't out of pure snobbery that I'd been buying *Cahiers* for the last two years, and that my friend from *lycée* Voltaire, Claude D., and I shared our amazed commentary. It wasn't pure caprice if at the beginning of every month I pressed my nose against the window of the modest bookshop on Avenue de la République. Seeing that beneath the yellow border, the black and white picture on the cover of *Cahiers* had changed was enough to set my heart racing. But I didn't want the shop-keep to tell me whether or not there was a new issue. I wanted to find out for myself and then coolly buy the magazine, in a neutral voice, as if I was buying a notepad. It never even occurred to me to subscribe: I liked the anxious wait. Whether buying, writing for, or editing *Cahiers*, I could always hang around out front since it was "my place."

There were a handful of us at the *lycée* Voltaire who were surreptitiously recruited into cinephilia. The date: 1959. The word "cinephile" was still cheerful, although it already had the pathological connotations and the stale aura that would little by little discredit it. As for me, I immediately despised those who were too normal and sneered at the "cinemathèque rats" we were on the verge of becoming—guilty of living cinema passionately and life by proxy. At the dawn of the 1960s, the world of cinema was still an enchanted one. On the one hand it had all the charms of a *parallel* counter-culture. On the other it had the advantage of already being developed with a heavy history, recognized values, Sadoul's typos (that insufficient bible),[1] jargon, persistent myths, battles of ideas, and wars between magazines. The wars were almost over and we were certainly arriving a little late, but not so late that we couldn't nourish the tacit project of making this *whole* history, which wasn't even as old as the century, our own.

Being a cinephile meant simply devouring *another* education parallel to that of the *lycée*, with the yellow *Cahiers* as the common thread and a few "adult" *passeurs*[2] who, with conspiratorial discretion, showed us that indeed there was a world to discover, and maybe nothing other than *the* world to live in. Henri Agel[3]—a literature teacher at *lycée* Voltaire—was one of these peculiar *passeurs*. To spare himself, as well as us, the burden of Latin lessons, he would put to a vote whether to spend an hour on Titus Livius or watch movies. The pupils who chose the movies often left the decrepit cine-club pensive and feeling tricked. Out of sadism and probably because he had the prints, Agel showed little movies designed to seriously open the students' eyes: Franju's *Le sang des bêtes* and in particular Resnais' *Nuit et brouillard*. Through cinema I learned that the human condition and industrial butchery were not incompatible and that the worst had just happened.

I imagine that Agel, who wrote "Evil" with a capital E, enjoyed watching the effects of this peculiar revelation on the teenagers' faces. There had to be a degree of voyeurism in his brutal way of transmitting, via the cinema, this gruesome and unavoidable knowledge that we were the first generation to fully inherit. Christian but not proselytizing, and a rather elitist militant, Agel was *showing*. It was one of his talents. He was showing because it was necessary, and because the cinematic culture at the *lycée*, for which he was campaigning, also meant a silent classification of students: those who would never forget *Nuit et brouillard* and the others. I wasn't one of the "others."

Once, twice, three times, depending upon Agel's whims and the number of sacrificed Latin lessons, I watched the famous piles of dead bodies, hair, glasses, and teeth. I listened to Jean Cayrol's despondent commentary recited by Michel Bouquet along with Hanns Eisler's music, which seemed ashamed of itself for existing. A strange baptism of images: *to comprehend at the same time that the camps were real and that the film was just.* And to understand that cinema (alone?) was capable of approaching the limits of a distorted humanity. I felt that the distances set by Resnais between the subject filmed, the subject filming, and the subject spectator were, in 1959—as in 1955—the only ones possible. Was *Nuit et brouillard* a "beautiful" film? No, it was a *just* film. It's *Kapo* that wanted to be a beautiful film and wasn't. And I'm the one who would never quite see the difference between the just and the beautiful—hence my rather "workaday" boredom in front of beautiful images.

Already captivated by cinema, I didn't need to be seduced as well. And there was no need to talk to me like a baby. As a child I never saw *any* Disney movies. Just as I went directly to communal school, I was proud to have been spared the infantile and clamorous kindergarten showings. Worse: animated movies for me would always be something other than cinema. Even worse: animated movies would always be something of an enemy. No "beautiful image," especially drawn, would match the emotion—fear and trembling—before *recorded* things. All of this, which is so simple, and took me years to formulate simply, began to come out in front of Resnais' images and Rivette's text. Born in 1944, two days before D-Day, I was old enough to discover *my* cinema and *my* history at the same time. A strange history that for a long time I believed I was sharing with others, before realizing, rather late, that it was well and truly mine.

What does a child know? Especially this child, Serge D., who wanted to know everything except that which concerned him? What absence *from the world* will later require the presence of images *of the world*? I know of few expressions more beautiful than Jean-Louis Schefer's in

L'homme ordinaire du cinéma when he speaks of "the films that have watched our childhood." It's one thing to learn to watch movies "professionally"— only to verify that movies watch us less and less—but it is another to live with those movies that watched us grow up and saw us—prematurely hostage to our coming biographies—already entangled in the snare of our history. For me, *Psycho*, *La Dolce Vita*, *The Indian Tomb*, *Rio Bravo*, *Pickpocket*, *Anatomy of a Murder*, *The Taira Clan*, or *Nuit et brouillard*, in particular, are unlike any other films. To the rather brutal question "Does this watch you?" all of them answer yes.

The corpses in *Nuit et brouillard* and then two years later those in the opening shots of *Hiroshima mon amour* are among those "things" that watched me more than I saw them. Eisenstein tried to produce such images, but it was Hitchcock who succeeded. It's only one example, but how can I ever forget the first meeting with *Psycho*? We snuck into the Paramount Opera theater without paying and the movie was terrorizing in the most normal way. Then, near the end of the film, my perception slides upon a scene, a careless montage out of which only grotesque props emerge: a cubist robe, a falling wig, and a brandished knife. From the collectively experienced fear follows a calm of resigned solitude: the brain functions as a second projector allowing the image to continue flowing, letting the film and the world continue without it. I can't imagine a love for cinema that does not rest firmly on the stolen present of this "continue on without me."

Who hasn't experienced this state or known these screen memories? Unidentified images are engraved in the retina; unknown events inevitably happen and spoken words become the secret code of an impossible self-knowledge. Just as Paulhan speaks about literature as an experience of the world "when we are not there" and Lacan speaks about "that which is missing from its place," these moments "neither seen nor taken" are the primitive scene of the lover of cinema, the scene *in which he wasn't present and yet it was entirely about him*. The cinephile? He who in vain keeps his eyes wide open but will tell no one that he *couldn't* see a thing; he who prepares himself for a life as a professional "watcher," as a way to make up for his tardiness, as slowly as possible.

Thus my life had its zero point, its second birth, which was experienced as such and immediately commemorated. The year is well known, again 1959. It is—coincidentally?—the year of Duras' famous "you saw nothing at Hiroshima." My mother and I left *Hiroshima mon amour*, both of us staggered—we weren't the only ones—because we never thought that cinema was capable of "that." On the subway platform I finally realized that to the tedious question I could never answer—"What are you going to do with your life?"— I had just found a response. "Later," one way or another, it would be cinema. And I never kept any details of this cinema-birth from myself: *Hiroshima*, the platform of the metro station, my mother, the now closed *Agricultures* theater and its seats will often be remembered as the legendary set of the good origin, the one you choose for yourself.

Resnais is the name that links this primitive scene in three acts over two years. It's because *Nuit et brouillard* was possible that *Kapo* was born obsolete and that Rivette could write his article. However, before becoming the prototype of the "modern" filmmaker, Resnais was just another *passeur*. If he was revolutionizing "cinematic language" (as we used to say), it's because he took his *subject* seriously and because he had the intuition, almost the luck, to recognize this subject among all the others: nothing less than the human species coming out of the Nazi camps and the atomic trauma, disfigured and ruined. There has always been something strange in the fact that later on I became a bored spectator of Resnais' other films. It seemed to me that his attempts to revitalize a world whose illness he alone had registered in time were destined to produce nothing but uneasiness.

Therefore I won't make the journey of "modern" cinema with Resnais, but rather with Rossellini. Nor will the moral lessons be memorized and conjugated with Resnais but instead with Godard. Why? First, because Godard and Rossellini spoke, wrote, and thought out loud while the image of Saint Alain Resnais freezing in his anoraks and begging us—rightly but in vain—to believe him when he said that he wasn't an intellectual started to get on my nerves. Was I "avenging" myself for the importance of two of his movies at the beginning of my life? Resnais was the filmmaker who kidnapped me from childhood or rather made me a *serious* child for three decades. And he is precisely the one with whom, as an adult, I would never share anything. I remember that at the end of an interview—for the release of *La vie est un roman*—I thought it a good idea to tell him about the shock I experienced with *Hiroshima mon amour*. He thanked me stiffly, as if I had just complimented him on his new raincoat. I was offended, but I was wrong: the films that have watched our childhood can't be shared, not even with their author.

Now that this story has come full circle and I've had more than my share of the "nothing" to be seen at Hiroshima, I inevitably ask myself: could it have been different? Facing the camps, was there any other possible justness besides the anti-spectacular *Nuit et brouillard*? A friend recently brought up the George Stevens' documentary made at the end of the war, which was buried, exhumed, and then shown on French television not so long ago. It is the first movie to record the opening of the camps in color, and the colors transform it—*without any abjection*—into art. Why? Is it the difference between color and black and white, between America and Europe, between Stevens and Resnais? What's amazing in Stevens' film is that it's the story of a journey: the daily progression of a small group of soldiers and filmmakers wandering across a destroyed Europe, from the ravaged Saint-Lô to Auschwitz, which nobody had foreseen and that totally overwhelms the entire crew. And then a friend tells me that the piles of dead bodies have a strange beauty which make her think of this century's great paintings. As always, Sylvie Pierre[4] was right.

What I understand today is that the beauty of Stevens' film is due less to the justness of the distance than to the *innocence* of the gaze. Justness is the burden of the one who comes "after," innocence the terrible grace accorded to the first to arrive, to the first one who simply makes the cinematic gesture. It took me until the mid-1970s to recognize in Pasolini's *Salo*, or even in Syberberg's *Hitler*, the other sense of the word "innocent": not so much the not-guilty but the one who in filming evil doesn't think evil. In 1959, as a young boy paralyzed by his discovery, I was already caught in the collective guilt. But in 1945, perhaps it was enough to be American and to witness, like George Stevens or Corporal Samuel Fuller at Falkenau, the opening of the real gates of the night, camera in hand. One had to be

American—that is to say, to believe in the fundamental innocence of the spectacle—to make the German population walk by the open tombs, to *show* them what they were living next to, so well and so badly. It took ten years before Resnais could sit down at the editing table and fifteen years before Pontecorvo made this one little move too many that revolted us, Rivette and I. Necrophilia was the price of this "delay" and was the erotic body double of the "just" gaze—the gaze of a guilty Europe, Resnais' gaze, and consequently mine.

This is how my story began. The space that Rivette's sentence opened was truly mine, as the intellectual family of *Cahiers du cinéma* was already mine. But I realized that this space wasn't so much a vast field as a narrow door. On the noble side was the *jouissance* of the just distance and its reverse, sublime necrophilia or necrophilia sublimated. On the not so noble side was the possibility of a completely other *jouissance* unable to be sublimated. It's Godard who, showing me videotapes of "concentration camp porn" tucked away in his video collection at Rolle, was surprised that nothing had been said about these films and that no interdiction had been pronounced. As if their creators' cowardly intentions and their viewers' trivial fantasies somehow "protected" them from censorship and indignation. Evidence that in the domain of sub-culture, the silent claim of an obligatory interlacing of executioners and victims was persisting. I was never really upset about the existence of these films. I had for them—just like any openly pornographic films—the almost polite tolerance one has for the expression of a fantasy that, so naked, claims only the sad monotony of its necessary repetition.

It's the other pornography that always revolted me: the "artistic" pornography of *Kapo*, or, a little later, *The Night Porter*, and other retro films of the 1970s. To this consensual after the fact aestheticization, I would prefer the obstinate return of the non-images in *Nuit et brouillard* or the unfurling drives of *Ilsa, She Wolf of the S.S.*, which I wouldn't see. At least these films had the honesty to acknowledge the impossibility of telling a story, the stopping point in the course of history, when storytelling freezes or runs idle. So we shouldn't be speaking about amnesia or repression but rather about foreclosure. Later I would learn the Lacanian definition of foreclosure: a hallucinatory return to the real of something upon which it was impossible to place a "judgment of reality." In other words: since filmmakers hadn't filmed the policies of the Vichy government, their duty fifty years later wasn't to imaginarily redeem themselves with movies like *Au revoir les enfants* but to draw the contemporary portrait of the good people of France who, from 1940 to 1942 (and that includes the Vel' d'Hiv raid[5]), didn't budge. Cinema being the art of the present, their remorse is of no interest.

This is why the spectator who I was before *Nuit et brouillard* and the filmmaker who tried to show the unrepresentable with this film were linked by a complicit symmetry. Either it's the spectator who is suddenly "missing from his place" and is stilled while the film continues, or it's the film which, instead of "continuing," folds back onto itself and onto a temporarily definitive "image" that allows the spectator to continue believing in cinema and the subject-citizen to live his life. Spectator-stilled, image-stilled: cinema entered adulthood. The sphere of the visible had ceased to be wholly available: there were gaps and holes, necessary hollows and superfluous plenitude, forever missing images and always defective gazes. The spectacle and the spectator stopped playing every ball. It is thus having chosen cinema—supposedly "the art of moving images"—that I began my cinephagic life under the paradoxical aegis of a first *image-stilled*.

This still protected me from strict necrophilia and I never saw any of the rare films or documentaries "on the camps" that came after *Kapo*. The matter was settled for me with *Nuit et brouillard* and Rivette's article. For a long time I have been like the French authorities, who, still to this day, in the face of any resurgence of anti-Semitism, urgently broadcast Resnais' film as if it is part of a secret arsenal that, whenever evil returns, can indefinitely apply its virtues of exorcism. If I didn't apply the axiom of the "tracking shot in *Kapo*" only to films that were exposed to abjection by their subject, it was because I was tempted to apply it to *every* film. "There are things," wrote Rivette, "that must be approached with fear and trembling. Death is undoubtedly such a thing, and how does one, at the moment of filming such a mysterious thing, avoid feeling like an impostor?" I agreed.

Since there are only a few films in which nobody dies, there were many occasions to fear and tremble. Indeed certain filmmakers weren't impostors. Again, in 1959, Miyagi's death in *Ugetsu* nailed me to the seat of the Studio Bernard theater. Mizoguchi filmed death as a vague fatality that one *saw* could and could not happen. The scene is memorable: in the Japanese countryside ravenous bandits attack travelers and one of them kills Miyagi with a spear. But he almost does it inadvertently, teetering, moved by a bit of violence or an idiotic reflex. This event seems so accidental that the camera almost misses it, and I'm convinced that all spectators of *Ugetsu* have the same crazy, almost superstitious idea that if the camera hadn't been so slow the event would have happened "out of frame," or who knows, it might not have happened at all.

Is it the camera's fault? In dissociating the camera-movement from the actors' gesticulations, Mizoguchi proceeded in precisely the opposite manner of *Kapo*. Instead of an embellished glance, this was a gaze that "pretended not to see," that preferred not to have seen and thus showed the event taking place *as an event*, that is to say, ineluctably and obliquely. An absurd and worthless event, absurd like any accident and worthless like war—a calamity that Mizoguchi never liked. An event that doesn't concern us enough to even move past it, shameful. I bet that at precisely this moment, every spectator of *Ugetsu absolutely* knows the absurdity of war. It doesn't matter that the spectator is a westerner, the movie Japanese, and the war medieval: it's enough to shift from pointing with the finger to showing with the gaze for this knowledge—the only knowledge cinema is capable of, as furtive as it is universal—to be given to us.

Opting so early for the panoramic shot in *Ugetsu* instead of the tracking shot in *Kapo*, I made a choice whose gravity I would only measure ten years later, amidst the late and radical politicization of *Cahiers* after 1968. If Pontecorvo, the future director of *The Battle of Algiers*, is a courageous filmmaker with whom I share by and large the same political beliefs, Mizoguchi seemed to have lived solely for his art and to have been a political opportunist. So where is the difference? Precisely in the "fear and trembling." Mizoguchi is scared of war for different reasons than Kurosawa: he is appalled by little men hacking each other apart for some feudal virility. It's this fear, this desire to vomit and flee, which issues the stunned panoramic shot. It's this fear that makes this moment just and therefore able to be shared.

Pontecorvo neither trembles nor fears: the concentration camps only revolt him ideologically. This is why he can inscribe himself in the scene with the worthless but pretty little tracking shot.

I realized that most of the time cinema oscillated between those two poles. With even more substantial directors than Pontecorvo, I often stumbled upon this smuggler's way of adding extra parasitic beauty or complicit information to scenes that didn't need it. It was thus that the wind blowing back the white parachute, like a shroud, over a dead soldier's body in Fuller's *Merrill's Marauders* troubled me for years. However, not as much as Ana Magnani's revealing skirt after she is shot dead in *Rome, Open City*. Rossellini was also hitting "below the belt," but in such a new way that it would take years to know towards which abyss it was taking us. Where does the event end? Where is the cruelty? Where does obscenity begin and where does pornography end? I knew these were questions constitutive of the "post-camp" cinema. A cinema that I began to call, because we were the same age, "modern."

This modern cinema had one characteristic: it was *cruel*; we had another: we accepted this cruelty. Cruelty was on the "good side." It was cruelty that said no to academic "illustration" and destroyed the counterfeit sentimentalism of a wordy humanism. Mizoguchi's cruelty, for instance, of showing two irreconcilable movements together, producing an unbearable feeling of "not helping someone in danger." A modern feeling *par excellence*, coming fifteen years before the long tracking shots in *Weekend*. An archaic feeling as well since that cruelty was as old as cinema itself, like an index of what was fundamentally modern in cinema, from the last shot in *Limelight* to Browning's *The Unknown*, and up to the end of *Nana*. How could one forget the slow, trembling tracking shot that the young Renoir hurls towards Nana lying on her bed, dying of smallpox? How is it that some people see in Renoir a crooner of the good life when he was one of the few filmmakers, right from the beginning, who was capable of finishing someone off with a tracking shot?

Actually, cruelty was within the logic of my journey at the combative *Cahiers*. André Bazin, who already theorized cruelty, had found it so closely linked to the essence of cinema that he almost made it "its thing." Bazin, the lay saint, liked *Louisiana Story* because you could see a bird eaten by a crocodile in real time and in one shot: cinematic proof and forbidden editing. Choosing *Cahiers* was choosing realism and, as I would discover, a certain contempt for imagination. To Lacan's formula "Do you want to watch? Then watch this" there was already the response of "Has it been recorded? Well then I have to watch it," even and especially when "it" was painful, intolerable, or completely invisible.

For this realism was two-faced. If modern filmmakers were showing a world surviving through realism, it was with a completely other realism—one more "realistic"—that movie propaganda in the 1940s had collaborated with the lies and foreshadowed death. This is why in spite of all it was fair to call the former realism, born in Italy, "neo." It was impossible to love the "art of the century" without seeing this art working with the madness of the century and being worked by it. Contrary to the theater, with its collective crises and cures, cinema, with its personal information and mourning, had an intimate relation with the horror from which it was barely recovering. I inherited a guilty convalescent, an old child, and a tenuous hypothesis. We would grow old together but not eternally.

Conscientious heir, a model *ciné-fils*,[6] with "the tracking shot in *Kapo*" as a protective charm, I didn't let the years go by without some apprehension: what if the talisman lost its power? I remember a course I was teaching at Censier[7] where I distributed Rivette's text to my students and asked for their impressions. It was still a "red" period when some students were trying to glean a bit of the political radicalism of '68 from their professors. It seemed that out of consideration for me the most motivated of them consented to see "On Abjection" as an interesting historical, but slightly dated document. I wasn't insistent with them, and if I ventured to repeat the experience with students today, I wouldn't be so concerned as to whether or not they understood the tracking shot, but I would have my heart set on knowing that they saw some *trace* of abjection. To be honest, I'm afraid they wouldn't. A sign that not only are tracking shots no longer a moral issue, but that the cinema is even too weak to entertain such a question.

Thirty years after the repeated projections of *Nuit et brouillard* at the *lycée* Voltaire, concentration camps—which served as my primitive scene—have ceased to be held in the sacred respect in which Resnais, Cayrol, and many others maintained them. Returned to the historians and the curious, the question of the camps is from now on linked with their work, their divergences, and their madness. The foreclosed desire, which returns "like a hallucination in the real," is evidently the one that should never have returned. It is the desire that no gas chambers, no final solution, or, at the most, no camps ever existed: revisionism, Faurissonism, negationism, sinister and last -isms. Film students today are not only inheriting the tracking shot in *Kapo*, but also an uncertain transmission, a poorly defined taboo, in brief just another round in the worthless history of the tribalization of the same and the fear of the other. The image-stilled has ceased to operate; the banality of evil can animate new, electronic images.

In contemporary France there are enough symptoms surging forth for someone of my generation to look back on the history he was given and notice the landscape he grew up in, a landscape that is both tragic and comfortable. Two political dreams defined by Yalta: American and Communist. Behind us was a moral point of no return symbolized by Auschwitz and the new concept of "crimes against humanity." Ahead of us, the unthinkable, almost reassuring, nuclear apocalypse. What had just ended lasted more than forty years. I belonged to *the first generation* for which racism and anti-Semitism had fallen definitively into the "dustbin of history." The first and only generation? The only one in any case which cried out so easily against fascism ("fascism will not pass!") because it seemed a thing of the past, once and for all, null and void. A mistake to be sure, but a mistake that didn't stop us from living very well during the "thirty glorious years,"[8] but in quotation marks. Naïve to be sure, acting as if Resnais' elegant necrophilia in the so-called "aesthetic" field would eternally keep any intrusion "at a distance."

"No poetry after Auschwitz," said Adorno, before rethinking this now famous formula. "No fiction after Resnais," I could have echoed before abandoning this slightly excessive idea. "Protected" by the shockwave produced by the discovery of the camps, did we now believe humanity had fallen into the inhuman only once with no chance of it happening again? Had we really bet that for once the worst was over? At this point did we hope that what wasn't yet called the Shoah was the *unique* historical event "thanks" to which *the whole of* himankind was "exiting" history in order to look at it from above and instantly recognize the worst face of its own possible fate? It seems we had.

But if "unique" and "the whole of" were too much and if humankind didn't inherit the Shoah as the *metaphor* of what it was and is capable of, then the extermination of the Jews would remain a Jewish story and also—in order of importance with regards to guilt, *by metonymy*—a very German story, a French story, and consequently an Arab story, but not very Danish and almost not Bulgarian at all. The "modern" imperative to articulate the image-stilled and pronounce the embargo on fiction responded to—within cinema—the possibility of the metaphor. The history of telling another story another way where "humankind" was the only character and the first anti-star. The history of giving birth to *another* cinema "which would know" that to give the event back to fiction too early is to take away its uniqueness, because fiction is this freedom which dissolves and opens itself beforehand to an infinity of variations and the seduction of true lies.

In 1989, while visiting Phnom Penh and the Cambodian countryside for *Libération*, I caught a glimpse of what genocide—that is, autogenocide—"looked like" when left without any images and almost no trace. Ironically, I saw the proof that cinema was no longer intimately linked to human history by the fact that, unlike the Nazi executioners who filmed their victims, the Khmer Rouge left behind only photographs and mass graves. Because another genocide—the Cambodian genocide—was left both imageless and unpunished, a retroactive effect of contagion occurred: the Shoah itself was rendered relative. Return of the blocked metaphor to the active metonymy, return of the image-stilled to the viral analogue. It went very quickly: in 1990 the "Romanian revolution" was frivolously indicting indisputable murderers for "illegal possession of firearms *and* genocide." Does everything need to be repeated? Yes everything, but this time without cinema—hence the mourning.

Undoubtedly we *believed* in cinema, which is to say we did everything not to believe it. That's the whole history of the post-'68 *Cahiers* and its impossible rejection of Bazinism. Of course it wasn't about "sleeping in the image-bed [*plan-lit*]" or upsetting Barthes by confusing the real and the representation. We knew too much not to put the spectator in the signifying concatenation or to locate the tenacious ideology beneath the false neutrality of technology. Pascal Bonitzer and I were even a little brave when we shouted in cracking voices before an amphitheater packed with excited leftists that a film could no longer be "seen" but had to be "read." It was a laudable effort to be on the side of the non-duped, laudable and, in my case, in vain. There always comes a moment when you have to pay your debt to the cash-box of sincere belief and *dare to believe in what you see.*

Of course you're not obligated to believe in what you see—it can even be dangerous—but you're not obligated to hold on to cinema either. There has to be some risk and some virtue, that is, some value, in the act of showing something to someone who is capable of seeing it. Learning how to "read" the visual and "decode" messages would be useless if there wasn't still the minimal, but deep-seated, conviction that *seeing* is superior to not seeing, and that what isn't seen "in time" will never really be seen. Cinema is an art of the present. If nostalgia doesn't suit it, it's because melancholy is its instantaneous double.

I remember the vehemence with which I said this for the first and last time. It was at a film school in Teheran. In front of the invited journalists, Khemais K. and myself, there were rows of boys with budding beards and rows of black sacks—probably the girls. The boys were on the left and the girls on the right, all in accordance with the apartheid. The most interesting questions—those from the girls—came to us on furtive little slips of paper. And seeing those girls so attentive and so stupidly veiled, I gave way to a rage with no particular object; it was directed less towards them than to all the powers that be, and for whom the visible is primarily what is read, i.e. what is permanently suspected of betrayal and reduced with the assistance of a chador or a police of signs. Encouraged by the unusual moment and place, I delivered a sermon in favor of the visual before a veiled audience who agreed.

Late anger, terminal anger. For the age of suspicion is well and truly over. One is only suspicious when a certain idea of truth is at stake. Nothing like that really exists today except among creationists and bigots, those who attack Scorsese's *Last Temptation* or Godard's *Marie*. The images are no longer on the side of the dialectical truth of "seeing" and "showing"; they have entirely moved over to the side of promotion and advertising, which is to say the side of power. It's therefore too late not to begin working on what's left: the golden and posthumous legend of what cinema once was, of what it was and what it could have been.

> Our work will be to show how individuals, gathered together in the dark, were stoking their imagination to warm up their reality—that was silent cinema; to show how they have let the flame go out to the rhythm of social conquest, satisfied to maintain only a very small fire—this is the talkie and the television in the corner of the room.

When he decided upon this program—just recently, in 1989—Godard the historian could have added "Alone, at last!"

As for me, I remember the exact moment when I knew that the axiom of "the tracking shot in *Kapo*" should be revisited and the homemade concept of "modern cinema" revised. In 1979, French television broadcast *Holocaust*, the American mini-series by Marvin Chomsky. We had come full circle, and I was sent back to square one. If in 1945 the Americans allowed George Stevens to make his astonishing documentary, they never broadcast it because of the cold war. Unable to "deal" with that story, which after all is not theirs, the American entrepreneurs of entertainment temporarily abandoned it to European artists. But with that story, *like every story*, they reserved the *right to buy it*, and sooner or later Hollywood and the television machine would dare to tell "our" story. It would tell it very carefully but it would sell it to us as another American story. So *Holocaust* would become the misfortunes that tear apart and destroy a Jewish family: there would be extras looking a little too fat, good performances, generic humanism, action, and melodrama. And we would sympathize.

It would therefore be only in the form of the American docu-drama that this history could escape the cine-clubs and could, via television, concern this servile version of the "whole of humanity" that is the global TV audience. The simulation-*Holocaust* was certainly no longer confronting the strangeness of a humanity capable of a crime against itself, but it remained obstinately incapable of bringing back the singular beings—each with a story, a face, and a *name*—who made up this history, who were the exterminated Jews. Rather it would be graphic art—Spiegelman's *Maus*—that later dared to make this salutary act of re-singularization. Graphic art and not cinema since it's true that American cinema hates singularity. With *Holocaust*, Marvin Chomsky brought back, modestly and triumphantly, our perennial aesthetic enemy: the good old sociological program with its well-studied cast of suffering specimens and its light-show of animated police sketches. We had come full circle and we had truly lost. The proof? It was around this time that Faurissonian[9] tracts started to circulate in France.

It took me twenty years to go from *my* "tracking shot in *Kapo*" to this irreproachable *Holocaust*. I took my time. The "question" of the camps, of my prehistory, would still and forever be put to me, but *no longer really through cinema*. Yet it was with cinema that I had understood in what respect this history concerned me and in which *form*—one tracking shot too many—it had appeared to me. We must remain faithful to the face that once transfixed us. And every "form" is a face that looks at us. This is why, even if I feared them, I never believed those at the *lycée* cine-club who condescendingly attacked those poor "formalist" fools who were guilty of preferring the personal *jouissance* of the "form" to the "content" of films. But only he who has been struck early enough by *formal violence* will end up realizing—at the end of his life—how this violence also has an "essence." And the moment will always come early enough for him to die cured, having traded the enigma of the singular figures of his history for the banalities of a "cinema as reflection of society" and other serious questions without answers. The form is desire, the essence but the background when we are no longer here.

These were my thoughts a few days ago while watching a music video on television that languorously interlaced famous singers with famished African children. The rich singers ("We are the world, we are the children!") were mixing their image with the image of the starving. In fact they were taking their place, replacing them, erasing them. Dissolving and mixing stars and skeletons in a kind of figurative flashing where two images try to become one, the video elegantly carried out this electronic communication between North and South. Here we have, I thought, the present face of abjection and the improved version of my tracking shot in *Kapo*. These are the images I would like at least *one* teenager to be disgusted by or at least *ashamed* of. Not merely ashamed to be nourished and rich, but ashamed to be seen as someone who *has to be aesthetically seduced* where it is only a matter of conscience—good or bad—of being a human and nothing more.

I realized that my entire history is there. In 1961 a camera movement aestheticized a dead body and thirty years later a dissolve makes the dying and the famous dance together. Nothing has changed, neither I—forever incapable of seeing in this a carnivalesque dance of death, medieval and ultra-modern—nor the predominant conceptions of consensual beauty. The form has changed a bit, though. In *Kapo*, it was still possible to be upset with Pontecorvo for inconsiderately abolishing a distance he should have "kept." The tracking shot was immoral for the simple reason that it was putting us—he as a filmmaker and I as a spectator—in a place where we did not belong. Where I anyway could not and did not want to be, because he "deported" me from my real situation as a spectator-witness, forcing me to be part of the picture. What was the meaning of Godard's formula if not that *one should never put oneself where one isn't nor should one speak for others*?

Imagining Pontecorvo's gestures deciding upon and mimicking the tracking shot with his hands, I am even more upset with him because in 1961 a tracking shot still meant rails, a crew, and physical effort. Yet I have more trouble imagining the movements of the person responsible for the electronic dissolve of "We are the World." I imagine him pushing buttons on a console, with the images at his fingertips, definitely cut off from what or whom they represent, incapable of suspecting that someone could be upset with him for being a slave to automatic gestures. That person belongs to a world—television—where, alterity having more or less disappeared, there are no longer good or bad ways to manipulate images. These are no longer "images of the other" but images among others on the market of brand images. And this world, which no longer revolts me, which provokes only lassitude and uneasiness, is precisely the world "without cinema." That is to say, without this feeling of belonging to humanity via *a supplementary country called cinema*. And then I clearly see why I have adopted cinema: so it could adopt me in return and could teach me to ceaselessly touch—with the gaze—that distance between myself and the place where the other begins.

Of course this story begins and ends with the camps because they are the limit that was awaiting me at the beginning of my life and at the end of my childhood. Childhood: it will have taken me a lifetime to win it back. This is why (message to Jean-Louis Schefer) I will probably end up seeing *Bambi*.

Part II

CHAPTER 2

Cine-biography

Before trying to conduct this interview chronologically, what strikes me about you, listening to and reading you, is the clarity of your experience with cinema, gathered today to such a concentrated point that you are able to create a perfect synthesis out of your biography and your theoretical, critical, and journalistic experience. There is something like a concentrated history, that of post-war cinema, which renders visible the development of cinema and the cinephile since your childhood.

There's an image that I really like; it's the rear-view mirror. There's a moment—let's call it aging or dying—when it's better to look in the rear-view mirror. Because ultimately there we can see the image of our past just as clearly as the way this image is modified by all of the presents, which we no longer look out for, which falls from the eyes like an ephemeral palimpsest, "dromoscopic." In the receding of the rear-view mirror, we look back at what this present resembled.

It's possible that for a long time, ten or twenty years, we've been led along a road that never stops turning. Instead of discovering the landscape that awaits us, we get the sense of covering an all too perfect spiral. Like the turn-off on a highway that we're afraid is a loop and not a spiral, and which will bring us back to our starting point. The result: no image before us, a single image behind us, the catch-all picture-frame in the rear-view mirror that ceaselessly recomposes itself. Result: the cult success of the little phrase I quoted in my first book: "As soon as he crossed the bridge, the phantoms came to meet him."

And apparently the phantoms are coming, in today's France, where, vexed and incredulous, I discover to what extent it distills the same old song from my childhood. Maybe it's only an illusion, dizziness from the never-ending spiral which steals us off to another landscape, and which has become the picture-frame of our life and legend. But, at the moment that I say this, there are children who are not looking in the rear-view mirror, but rather through the windshield, and who have a very clear sense of their linear progress in the landscape they are facing. The eternal return of the becoming conscious of the eternal return.

When did this effect of the spiral and the rear-view mirror become clear for me? Probably when I started working at *Libération*, which is to say, rather late. It's likely that there are other moments on the spiral which pass very close to the place we left, the place of birth, and that we recognize, from slightly higher up, but close enough that we want to touch it. I used to say rather audaciously that I was born at the same time as what I call modern cinema, grown-up cinema, the cinema of Rosellini when he made *Rome, Open City*. It's almost a mnemotechnique: I tell myself I am the same age as modern cinema, a little less than 50 years old … already. And we won't grow old together. It's no less true that I preferred to come to the world in another country, Italy, and in a fundamental counter-time, when something of the innocence of cinema had already been reached and would never return. It was Italy, not France. I had no desire to know French disenchantment, like *Le Corbeau*, for example, which I must have only seen once.

Le Corbeau *made its mark on people like Truffaut, Rohmer, or even our friend Jean Douchet, a whole generation who must have been between 10 and 15 years old during the war, and for whom the film corresponded to a certain disgust with the adult world: anonymous letters, informing, and moral treason. What would it mean to become a part of the cinema when one saw* Le Corbeau *at the age of 12?*

I think that for me the affair was settled and the Clouzot of the 1950s was one of those adults who affected disgust with the depravity of the adult world, while they were—at least in the eyes of children—its typical representatives. Clouzot, no more so than Duvivier, Autant-Lara or any others, was unable to lay claim to Bernanos' magnificent phrase at the beginning of *Grands Cimetières sous la lune*: "What importance has my life? I only want it to remain faithful until the end to the child I was … , the child I was and who is now like a grandfather to me." People like me who are the children of their work, who have to construct for themselves the story of their origin, who can't allow themselves to lose the thread of their lives—even if dreamt-up or rigged—these people feel in a very "raw" way the imposture of the disenchanted professionals. And this imposture is a French specialty, very comfortable, very bourgeois.

So, to answer the question, that's why this spiral effect, this effect of "everything is there," available, thinkable, handy, happens more frequently with me. I have this strange privilege of having never been angry with my childhood, of wanting to trade it for something else, to bargain with it or to lose it. I've had enough leisure time to endlessly re-tell myself the story of my life, according to the interests of my successive presents and according to this logic of the rear-view mirror which makes us adapt what we were still thinking yesterday about the past to a new and unforeseen element which forces us to reinterpret everything. Through a kind of hindsight I ended up giving off the strange feeling that a history had passed through me, the history of our collective passivity as cinephilic children. Spoiled children or lost children? I still waver, I go back and forth between them. The first beneficiaries of the peace—that of Yalta—or the last victims of the war—those we hear in their mothers' bellies?

Recently, I reproached Bertrand Blier for his bright idea of the "student's parent." I detest student's parents. I'm always for the lone kid like I was, never for his parents. At the communal school I worked hard, regularly received honors, and my mother didn't have to keep an eye on my schoolwork. At the exit of École Keller[1] I saw the anxious, conniving mothers melting before the teachers in grey blouses, haggling with them over the valuation of the flesh of their flesh. I was proud that my mother didn't have to be a "student's parent." Since I worked hard, it seemed natural to dispense with it. I was convinced that she wouldn't have liked talking about me with a teacher behind my back. That would have been a betrayal. Just as I could never stand when someone spoke about someone else in the third person when that person was right there, in flesh and blood, able to respond.

I think I maintained that with cinema as well. First the desire to be an adult as soon as possible. Then, a sort of gratitude towards my mother, who never thought for a second that I should see "children's films" and with whom I made a deal very early on: she consented to go with me to see "cloak-and-sword" films, and I would go to melodramas with her. In fact, I think we both had a relationship to cinema that was strongly colored by Italy.

Did you work hard precisely to avoid the abusive mothering of "students' parents" who demand high status for their offspring? Did you want to avoid being "betrayed" on this terrain?

Probably. I had to maintain this very particular feeling of alliance I had with my mother—an alliance that was *ideological avant la lettre*—of a young, fatherless boy who made common cause with his single mother against all the wounds and cuts that society was capable of. Of course I was very close to my mother, physically, incestuously so, etc. And at the same time this proximity had a logic, the logic of an eventual combat against the moral order, against normal people, against the worthless and collaborating France that a child like myself *felt certain* would never be his country. In fact I was my mother's ally in a potential fight that never really took place because of the changing mores. Likewise, I was always ready to go to war against social conformity, the moral order, and all the things that I only knew through the books and literature of the nineteenth century, but which—even if I was always scared of them—I never had to endure. There is a kind of "Tartar Steppe"[2] in my anxious vigilance.

At what point did it begin to formulate itself like this?

Definitely late. But it's always late when we finally discover the words to say "it." There were only women around my cradle: my mother, my grandmother, and my aunt. My grandmother partially raised me and I had another kind of alliance with her, quite different, simultaneously playful and cultural. Very early, in that house where there were at the most ten books, I relayed—by my simple existence as a good little male who went to school—my grandmother's old desire for social climbing. This desire had been pretty much trampled on and kept in the dark during her melodramatic and miserable life, but it never disappeared. My grandmother and I cultivated ourselves at the same time. Me at 12 years old and she at 50. She bought an old dive at Villepinte, which at the time was still pretty wild, and I sat astride my bike near the corner bookstores where "Le Livre de Poche"[3] had just started its collection and where you could find those cheap little books about great painters, which I collected.

[txt]My mother, forcing out cries of ecstatic complicity, always remained profoundly outside of that. It took a long time for me to understand that my mother was a real dunce, a little like Straub and Huillet's "enfant Ernesto":[4] secretly revolted by the idea that we want her to learn something which she doesn't know. This didn't stop her from reading in the subway her entire life, or from falling asleep under her book and immediately forgetting everything she read. As a child placed in the care of a nurse at La Sarthe, my mother understood that there was no reason to study since there was no one—certainly not her own mother, who had raised her very strictly—to whom that would give any pleasure. Today, although it obviously irritates me, I kind of admire my mother's beautiful determination not to learn anything. All the more beautiful since she aligns herself with a discourse where knowledge and culture are valorized.

My grandmother relived her life through culture. She always wanted to know at what age artists had died (he "died young") and above all if "they had known success during their lifetime." The feeling of being, ourselves, "the little people" was very present, yet happily affirmed, as if that put us on the level of these "great men" of the past, many of whom had been as poor as we were. There wasn't much resentment in our bulimic knowledge. We had tons of "little classics," Larousse, Vaubourdolle, Hatier, which scrolled through the history of French literature, filled with the faces of great writers and anecdotes about Malherbe or Fontenelle that entered into our personal folklore. We bought them from a peddler of large volumes of little character (some pages were blank, unprinted) like *Les Mystères de Paris* that we read aloud, with Rodolphe, Chouette and above all Chourineur.

We created a link between my grandmother's popular culture—Zola, the lyric works, Faust, operettas, Massenet, *Sur la mer calmé-e*—and what was to be mine, starting with cinema. The most amazing thing is that the link was made and to this day my grandmother absolutely never confuses Mizoguchi with Ozu.

During those years we were the rather happy poor, and I remember those times at the end of the month when there wasn't a dime in the house, we would empty the white buffet drawer of its long-forgotten coins, and my grandmother and I would go wait for my mother at métro Voltaire. We would see her come out of the station, and she would make either a negative gesture, meaning she hadn't gotten paid, or, on the contrary a gleeful one, which meant she was rich and that we were going to celebrate. I felt the sense of unity among the three of us very strongly, the obligation to find our own way, and the refusal to report to anyone as if that was our sovereignty. We were below, certainly, but apart. That's why I never suffered from poverty. It made its way into me but I didn't suffer. To be part of a tribe capable of laughing at its lot and hastily piecing together its survival seemed the most humanly important to me. I haven't really changed that much. Later I continued to prefer companions on the road over knowing whether or not the road was the path to success. This always allowed me to be sympathetic to the cause of others. For me, having inherited *absolutely no* political culture, to be on the left is undoubtedly this rather comic paternalism. I implicitly lived out my fate as a fatherless child, a vaguely heroic choice that put me "elsewhere." In any case I wouldn't have tolerated anyone pleading my case or taking up my cause. On the other hand, my normal bourgeois friends with bullying fathers, and suffocating mothers, found in me a confidant and an ally of steel who always took their side against the abject *pater familias*. But to be one's own lawyer? Never. The matter was settled, which is to say, forbidden.

During your childhood, what story was told in private, between your mother and you, or between your grandmother and you, about the subject of your birth, about this origin that you inherited?

Alright, I have to talk about the father, about my father, about the legend of my father. Because it's a legend that my mother, as well as the rest of the family, instilled in me from the beginning and which I never found anything wrong with throughout my life. All the same there is a reality behind it, someone who existed, who lived, who was old enough to be my mother's father, and who came from another world, from such an *elsewhere* that I saw myself spending my life alone with an atlas, going to look elsewhere to see if he was there! But as always the facts were more banal. My father's name was Pierre Smolensky, a Central European Jew, born or raised in Vienna in an important family and he had a brother who was a minister of state. In the legend told by my mother—ruthlessly recounted exactly the same, with exactly the same words—this man brightened the life of the three women for a period of time, and, if I understand right, was a sort of adventurer about whom nobody knows very much. He lived in America, established a home there—I thus have half-brothers in the United States—and, convinced that the Germans would win the war, he wanted to return there with my mother and me as soon as I was born. In one of the two photos that exists of him, he is a man of the past, well-dressed, wearing a hat, a character from between the wars, a made man. He ended up taking this young girl into his protection, my 17-year-old mother, who worked as an assistant in a seamstresses' studio, a studio where he had some interests. For my mother the war was the best time of her life: she was leaving her mother's sphere, she was allowed her caprices, she learned some English, stenography, she went to restaurants and the theater, the banks of the Marne, and to Ris-Orangis. She neither saw nor understood anything of the war, or of the occupation, and she obviously asked no questions. My father must have been Jewish since he was arrested by the French police near the end of the war. But since he had German friends, perhaps support, he didn't have to wear a yellow star.

I eventually realized that this legend played the role of a kind of Ten Commandments. I believed every single word, signifier by signifier. My mother would say to me, "Pierrot, your father went to every country in the world." She would also say, "He spoke every language." The result: I developed a strong taste for travel, and as soon as I could, I began collecting stamps in my passport, with this infantile, idiotic, idea that I could set foot in *all the countries of the world*. Evidently, I was pretty good with languages, imitating them rather well, and starting to learn all of them, rather casually. For a number of years I studied Chinese on my own: I used to calm my nerves with a few pages of calligraphy.

But above all, my father was also "in" the cinema, where he had the stage-name Pierre Sky. My mother explained that he was in "post-synchronization" and that he often dubbed for Albert Préjean in the Franco-German co-productions between the wars. He might have even had some small roles in films such as Christian-Jacque's *Premier bal*, or *Mam'zelle Nitouche*. In any case, here, too, my choice of cinema was inscribed in the legendary past of my father transformed by the desire of my mother.

She never stopped churning out, in the exact same words, the official *story* of her happiness and my luck. She was rather successful: indeed the place of my father would never be occupied by anyone else. Even she had to renounce it, and I remained the loyal offspring of this law that numbed the two of us, two biological children sharing the same fantasy, agreeing to have it in common. Occasionally, my mother seemed to discover another piece of the saga, as if she'd never said it before, thus it became, word by word, a canonical tale. The only thing she "forgot" to tell me was that my father was Jewish. She told me much later at a time when I was able to hear it, having in a sense always known, but much too late to enter into the story of my choice, to that of the century and of the others.

So that simplified everything.

Yes. Here's where I link-up with the "The Tracking Shot in *Kapo*" prolog. It's amazing how we always know, but with a more or less unconscious knowledge, all there is to know. On the one hand, I wasn't overly zealous: no investigation, no personal search for the father behind the wall of words, the fifty sentences of the official story, to find out all that my mother hadn't told me. And on the other hand, from a very young age, before even knowing that there was a "Jewish Question," I had the feeling that those images, the ones in *Nuit et brouillard*, were about me, that they watched me. All my life I lived with those corpses that cinema gave me, entrusting their existence to me, and at the same time, the cinema came out and opened itself before my eyes, like the instant that knows, that shows and knows, and that is irrefutable.

The cinema, the place of the dead father, was also a counterbalance to the discourse of the living mother. And little by little it appeared to me that the cinema was the place of the dead father to such an extent that it became comic. *A Season in Hell* has always been for me a personal reference book, and in this text there is a little phrase that always accompanied me: *I wasn't born to become a skeleton*. Oh yeah?! I was wrong.

In the cinema of my adolescence, in the cinema discovered practically alone at the school's cine-club, in the way forbidden books or slightly arousing medical texts helped develop a religion about sex, I *saw*. I saw, and in a sense I never returned from this vision. I saw my father die in the camps, and me, his posthumous mime, destined to become just as emaciated in my own time from AIDS. I, too, was therefore born to become that image, "to become a skeleton." On the one hand, I didn't allow myself "to say" that I was. On the other, I saw in the cinema, as one sees in coffee grounds, the face of my destiny. The image is probably just that: that which *goes without saying*.

I could have found my father behind Albert Préjean or in *Premier bal* or in *Mam'zelle Nitouche* or in a complete filmography under his pseudonym (Pierre Sky). He belonged to the film world twice: once in a small speaking part, and once as a corpse. It took me a while to develop this idea that "modern" cinema, born the same time as I was, was the cinema of a kind of *knowledge* of the camps, a knowledge that changed the ways of making cinema. I don't claim to have been the only one to discover this at my birth, or the only one to have participated in the adventure and risk of this knowledge. Today things close themselves almost impeccably, a page turns itself without me.

But during your childhood, was the relationship with your mother based on silence or words?

At the base of this story, the one that became law, my mother and I shared the same *father*, the one she didn't know: she as the last woman, essentially a child, he had made happy, and I as the proud offspring coming from this story, from this man, from this elsewhere of which one of the names was *cinema*. Obviously, if I tell this story today to people who are indifferent or even irritated by "cinephilia," it creates a pretty heavy effect, so heavy that, emboldened by my "olden days," I speak about movies as if they were beings with which one could have filial relationships. In order to remain in the desire of the mother, I had to proceed to an ultimately delirious montage: to be a cinephile, *ciné-fils*, a child of the cinema, mythologically born many times in such and such a film, since it is in this world, in this cinematic *limbo*, that, neither dead nor living, my father's body roamed as a phantom whom no one had given a grave, just like in a Greek tragedy.

One day my mother told me there was a film on TV with Préjean that she thought my father might have made an appearance in. I didn't watch the film. She did, but didn't see him. I had to spend part of my life knowing that he was etched, embedded, embalmed (how could I have been anything other than Bazinian?) in black and white films between the wars, and afraid of one day stumbling upon his celluloid face, beneath his dead eyes staring at me. At the same time, to keep the perverse contract with the mother alive, I never stopped leaving, in films or in life, on the map or on the terrain, as if I was following an endless mission: traveling near and far, going to Melun, Shanghai, and returning as if nothing happened; returning to Paris like Trenet's song *Revoir Paris, revoir les quais de la Seine*, a song which moreover very clearly specified *Ma mere m'attend* [my mother waits for me]. Seen from this angle, my travels are the story of my eternal return to Taillandiers, *nothing in the hands, nothing in the pockets*, with my mother, who was used to seeing me come and go, who prepared a fine ratatouille and did the dirty laundry. And I hear myself saying, as if I said it, the little phrase that underpins this whole ritual: *No, I didn't see him.*

But your father wasn't at all involved in cinema the way you were: he, actively, a little like a bricoleur *or an adventurer, you more fully, as a literary passion that was never mixed up with filmmaking.*

Cinema was simply the place you had to be. Not to make something there, but to be "there," to be at home there, more at home than in my home. People are surprised when I tell them that I never had the (conscious) desire to make films. I think it was in 1967 that I made a very masochistic short called *Une (très) mauvaise journée*, which I never finished. It was at a time when everyone around me was preparing to pass over to "the other side" of the camera, as we used to say. And I, who did pretty well on "this side" (since for me the cinema was and still is "the place of the other," a very particular other, that remains there like in a house of mirrors), put in my last two cents and made the cinematic gesture! That little shoot is a bad memory, a sort of ignoble nightmare. It was the certainty of being led onto the wrong stage, or at least not my stage. Then came 1968, which, for me, rendered all of that ridiculous.

As long as I've known you, I never would have guessed that this was your story. What I find striking is that you always wanted to avoid the scenario of a "big reunion" through a novel, a film, some sort of writing, an account, something that would allow you to reap the benefits of the legend. You preferred to take a line of flight, to go a little further for this meeting with the father.

I made the pleasure, and the anxiety, last a long time: never ceasing to leave, never ceasing to return, always putting off until tomorrow the moment when you have to confront something, or someone. So of course why not undergo psychoanalysis? Etc.

But you did your analysis with cinema.

That analysis took thirty years. In my case it was extremely slow, so dwelled upon that today I can say that "I die cured," that is to say, I recover the images which, as Jean-Louis Schefer says, "watched my childhood," the images of a disaster, but a disaster that was also a sign of choice, of levity: *our* choice, mine as well as cinema's. Cinema, the paradoxical art, privileged unlike the others. Cinema, the place of absent, dead fathers, for a generation or two of cinephiles to come, and I'm the most obstinate, riveted to my own "history" like a mollusk to a rock.

I sometimes wonder if the idea of "the death of cinema," which had its shining moment about ten years ago (via Wenders' films), wasn't for me the condition under which I might be able to write and live of my own accord. It was as if the cinema had to disappear, to pass from obscurity to the stage, from night to day, from fog to light, or just from "we" to "I." In fact, most ironically, it's my death that might ultimately be in synch with cinema's. If I was born the same year as *Rome, Open City*, it's good that at least this part of cinema that I was contemporaneous with will disappear with me: the thirty glorious years of modern cinema. This aspect of "after me, the deluge ..." should frustrate more than a few, as if we, the almost 50-year olds of today, were finally representing a senseless egoism, a sort of successful incest which ultimately lacked the desire to transmit something. Sometimes I tell myself that my lifetime, my own *timing* of myself, and that of cinema, fit each other pretty well: it took thirty years to turn a certain page, from Rossellini to the death of Pasolini. Thirty years is more or less what I was given as an active life. The cinema never abandoned me, like jazz for example. I believe that jazz is the most beautiful music of the century and I listened to it quite a lot. But the day Albert Ayler died I knew (in any case I decided) that the adventure was over, and that I wasn't going to become an old grandpa with my discophilic treasures: Wardell Gray's solo alongside Bird on "Scrapple from the Apple," or Sonny Rollins' on "Blue Seven." Not too long ago I watched Eastwood's *Bird* on television and I burst into tears just hearing Parker on the soundtrack. In the end, jazz, like cinema, was *someone*. Not a cultural domain amongst the others, but a fate almost comparable to that of a man, with all of its grandeur and triviality. One day cinema will have surpassed the century and then it will be finished with this odd parallelism, which is also a *promiscuity* that belongs to us (to me), between the time of the life of a man and the age of cinema. My grandmother told me about Feuillade's films which she had seen as a child, of *La main qui étreint*, which was for me even more terrifying than "la main-quétrin."[5]

What sort of alliances or friendships did that motivate you to have during your school days?

Those are effectively the right words: "alliance," "friendship." I never imagined that I could have any other sort of relationship with people other than one based on friendship. Friendship—the idea, or categorical imperative, of friendship—covered everything, including sex. But it's stronger than me: even when in Harrar, the city of Rimbaud, I meet little Abddullahi, a 15-year-old boy, who is as clever as a monkey, I consider him to be a friend as well, that is to say, an equal. Otherwise, it's simply prostitution. But again, when I see another boy, in Manila, a young prostitute named Dany with a tattoo on his right buttock, put his clothes back on and put my money in his underwear, I feel a sense of equality, of empathy which paves the way. I'm capable of criminal indifference, but not sneering cynicism.

I remember my first day at school—elementary school because I didn't go to nursery school—and the way that I became friends with another boy my age named Michel. It was already the question of the day: Who's to be a friend? Who's to be an enemy? A child's wisdom is extraordinary. He knows that he's not going to be one of the loud-mouths that dominate the playground, that he doesn't want to mess with those guys, and that he has to ignore the bullies in order to have sublime friendships. Definitely a *defensive* attitude.

Michel and I went every year to La Foire du Trone. It was a true event. We rode the bumper cars and our pleasure mainly consisted of not being bumped into! I was thinking about this period and I thought that perhaps I was completely in love only once in my life, and it was with Michel: we were about 7 or 8 years old. I would go play at his house on rue Keller, and we would play the most miserable games without toys, just codes that we made up. I never again had that feeling of time stopping, of a remaining abundance: there's just one person there who fulfills all the possible roles and horizons. As they say in the cantata: *Ich habe genug*, which means *I have enough*.

That was the absolute alliance, absolute security, due to the fact that we were two, united like the two halves of an hourglass. Obviously there was always this idea of *genug* in my later alliances, even and especially with *Cahiers du cinéma*, with some nevertheless very mitigated results. There is always this child's gaze at his peers on the playground: who will I be a friend with this year?

What does it mean that you weren't "strong in composition"? A will not to conform to the model of an enthusiastic student?

I was a very good student at school, pretty good at *lycée*, but I was terribly lazy and scattered. Besides, it seems to me that the environment that reigned at the *lycée* Voltaire wasn't great and the dominant ideology was resolutely secular, egalitarian, and ultimately "meritocratic." Ultimately I'm rather grateful for that education, "strict but just." This "meritocracy"—which never let go of me—was driven into me there. I was a student of the state, a grantee. I was a child rescued from the common people, adopted by the bourgeoisie, and I'm sure I didn't want to disappoint.

It's awful, but I never stopped "believing" in merit, even with all the "I know, but still ..." (*je sais bien, mais quand même*)[6] of denial. I'm still revolted by unrecognized merit. It always had a grand finale, the distribution of prizes and rewards, that of *Cela s'appelle* l'aurore,[7] and I always thought I was a part of this scene. There'd better be someone or something there that is able to *recognize* you! Today, with my illness, I don't have enough time to be polite, so I ask my friends to help me store *what belongs to me*. But all my life I functioned pretty well in the system that made me compassionate for the misfortune of my rich friends, friends whom I would have killed if they had shown even a gram of pity or paternalism.

Which is to say that around my friends at high school I improvised the part of the "protector" of the most deprived, crippled, and ugliest ducklings. And since I was actually too weak to protect them myself, I played the role of the sympathetic one who wouldn't exclude them. Still, I had a rather crazy conception of the relationship between the mental and the physical: I was friends with monsters because I was convinced there was *no* relationship between the personality, which was the only truth, and the body, which was wholly false. Another version of the arbitrary sign, like the map and the territory. It was a very, if not too, radical way of always already having moved past the questions of exclusion and racism—including what I could have suffered—by disqualifying physical appearances to such a point that there would be nothing left to exclude. However, I could always exercise a completely infinite and disinterested curiosity on an unlimited number of different "I"s.

Later, this would become part of "the vision of the world" of the great auteurs who interested me, *even before* I was reconciled with the actors' bodies. In effect, I imagine that if I'd developed a love of French actors, like Albert Préjean for example, what was I risking? Falling too quickly for the image that would break the charm. But there too I think that the choice of cinema, or, if you will, the "solution of cinema," came just in time to reinforce this meritocracy, this equality of things. When I was young, the cinema seemed to me to be the social *par excellence*, to make a film was to wildly manipulate the world, others, money, and language. Today I'm convinced that in spite of its horrible commercial tendencies, the cinema was and remains a world more democratic than all the rest of the arts. I imagine that the power relationships, the jealousies, the low blows, the injustices, have all become more terrible in the arts, which, having been modern for a while now, are no longer submissive to the triviality of public judgment, or to its immense capacity for indifference and negligence, its sacred selfishness and the resentment of the artists themselves. I have often raved about the cruelty of cinema without seeing that this cruelty had its opposite—Mizoguchian—compassion. Today, in the light of cinema, I see a space of reconciliation, a path to atonement.

Of course it all depends on which door we use to enter the home. I entered cinema, the home of the father, by a door I chose as soon as I saw it: the door of *Cahiers du cinéma*. You can say what you want about *Cahiers*, you can say all the bad things you like, but if there's a point in common with those whom it profoundly affected and those who created it, it's a complete or partial lack of social know-how and ambition. It didn't offer much. *Cahiers* never helped anyone "succeed," or rather to get quickly to a point beyond the agonizing shores of management, or maintenance, like Truffaut I suppose, who respected social success but who very quickly bore only its burden and sad responsibility. Choosing *Cahiers* was to choose beforehand all the horrors, tribulations, and adolescent terrors of an *institution* which already had its own history, a history with chapters still to be added. But it was definitely saving a certain candor regarding social traps, professional mores, the hypocritical billing and cooing, the annual end of the year dinner, the tension in the elevator and the backstabbing. It seems to me today that this candor is itself quite candid, but it is without a doubt the condition by which the journal endured and continues to endure.

Likewise when I was at the *Libération* of 1981, it was still a journal that one "believed" in. No advertising and a fixed salary of 5,000 francs.

I had a three-month trial period, I came in through the back door, forced to prove myself at 37 years old. That went well with my meritocratic ideals. Today I think that it must have allowed a lot of people to feel towards me that friendly contempt that normal people reserve for those who are "above it all" or for whom "it's good that people like that exist"—a sentence behind which I always heard a true desire for death. But I didn't suffer from what I barely understood. It's now that, indirectly, my pride complains a bit. But I could have never done *otherwise*. I said of the cinema that I had to be there, but in that strange balcony where, with a sort of disinterest, a child's seriousness, we watch the result *without fear*, the rush of images of the world the way it is, such that we don't want to take its path: a place where there are no choir-boys but only the rough laws of the social, money, treason, time, power, the rationality of the state of the studio, or of the artist, etc. I was part of that audience of choir-boys who were confronted early on with a certain tragic gravity of the spectacle that cinema offered. This innocence was quickly exposed; it is perhaps the ideal, perverse story that I tell myself. I find that things are now reversed: a no longer innocent audience is pretty savvy before the advertising of a feeble and sold-out cinema.

If I made the little boy in *Night of the Hunter* one of my favorite alter egos—the other being John Mohune in *Moonfleet*—it was because he was about 10 years old when the film was made in 1955, and therefore exactly one of my contemporaries, my "American" brother. The way that under Laughton's direction the little boy maintained the gaze of a gravity which he is as of yet unaware (all he knows is that he has to watch over his sister, and she knows nothing except that she is a girl), this wide-eyed gaze of those who don't know how to play their part, the amateur children who are nothing but little monkeys for adults: that's the legend in which I want to figure, it's the face that I like to think cinema gave to me, like a photographic image that took twenty years to develop.

Many became filmmakers for these same reasons: to avoid getting hit. That's what Truffaut wrote about Hitchcock, where the physical fantasy, the fear of being pushed around—with this primal scene of the police station where his father takes him to frighten him—is what made him take refuge in cinema. You found refuge in writing about cinema.

There's something in the act of "making" cinema that I don't have: the desire to impose oneself. Not out of virtue but out of the inability to bet on oneself, to believe in oneself. I believed in my destiny, a kind of pale star, but I didn't believe in me. As a *passeur* I stayed in the middle of the fjord, waiting for one of the banks to call me, or to take me by the hand, and since that never happened I began to send little messages, both written and oral, giving news from one bank to the other without myself belonging to either of them. I wasn't on the side of the normal people who laughingly consume movies, nor was I on the side of the specialists, of the doers, the artists, whose experience will end up proving that they too are very normal, which is to say, that there isn't much point in idealizing them.

I stayed in the middle of the fjord so long that I ended up—it's happening to me today—scheming, becoming part of the landscape, like a rather dignified scarecrow or a modern art statue. I waited patiently for someone to *see me*, and since I was incapable of making myself seen, I waited for a few to venture over to my side, the side of cinema, which is the only one in which I can exist favorably, and as soon as they showed up I overwhelmed them with all that I had never been able to tell anyone. I never had to produce evidence of my existence or of my value because the key to my existence was under the watch of the cinematic house of mirrors, with a prisoner for a father, and my value was what my mother gave me at my birth. What value? Zero value, simply that I exist.

We've come full circle: a nearly stillborn child, idle, born to become a "skeleton" and to represent *in extremis* the collective figure of a bizarre passion, a Bazinian saint, a *passion* that alas we can only dress up in the name of an illness: cinephilia, which here I try to report on from behind the scenes, except that this nebulous backstage is starting to create a lot of chasms.

I think we should welcome with humor what creates itself *starting from the place of the other*—to *its* place if I am its reverse. What I did voluntarily in my life never resulted in anything and caused only a vague throbbing anxiety in me. On the other hand, on two or three occasions I easily did things that weren't idiotic and that brought a bit of happiness to myself and others. Let's say that I worked just enough, and without order, care, or discipline, so that the way in which I was

at the same time worked upon wouldn't send me to the asylum. If there is "merit" in the final analysis of art, it is impure: it is a hybrid made up of conscious courage (working) and unconscious submission (being worked). If one of the two is missing, everything tips: courage alone becomes the mad power of work but the work of a slave, whereas submission alone becomes capable of imploding in its madness.

I always valorized what I didn't do: the personal work. I probably played the part well in the "throes" of solitary creation, as if the whole world knew or had known the anxiety of the blank page, the rage of expression, or the experience of limits. Just recently I was thinking that Cocteau was probably right in advising that we should always do what we are reproached for, because that's where we are, but the dyed-in-the-wool moralists, the Christians, the clerics—to whom I belong—don't want to hear about that: genius' tranquil arrogance and facility will make them sick, and they'll wait however long it takes for it to become bitter, to turn rotten, and in doing so humanize it.

Your story is coherent because today you're creating an exact synthesis out of it. But I wonder if what makes it possible for someone to write their own story is saying to oneself: here is what I wasn't, for example a jouisseur, *a hedonist, or an adept at happiness. I'm thinking for example of our friend Jean Douchet, who meant a lot to you at the time of your joining* Cahiers, *whose story is without a doubt very different.*

Jean is a bourgeois on the run who remained faithful to his codes, and to a certain moral pleasure *à la* Sacha Guitry. Those are the people who in general we refer to as hedonists. I did it with something else, with another *being of class*. Someone who would never own anything, who detested the idea of ownership, who truly owned nothing in the world, except for books and records, in short someone who could only own *himself* and experience the simple pleasures—the obtaining of pleasure itself being work—or simple happiness. And from such an absolutely basic simplicity comes a certainty, that by sharing these pleasures you simply belong to the human race, with those who, as my mother used to say, are "happy to live and to see clearly" (nice plan for a cinephile, by the way). It's something that I think about a lot now, with a sort of obstinate gratitude, as in Rossellini's *Fioretti*. Without a doubt it's a Franciscan sentiment, a walker's liveliness, incomprehensible to those who don't walk. "I sit, a leper, at the foot of a wall eaten away by the sun"—always Rimbaud, Rimbaud the walker.

All over the third world I made sure to sit leaning against the wall, in the middle of the day, being careful not to be disruptive, and I was definitely happy everywhere. The sun on the walls of Paris, "tomorrow is another day," the laziness of the lizard who always defers until tomorrow the pleasure of counting off in one's head the first twenty shots of a film in order to know if I'm in "my place." It's a happiness that's too modest not to be absolute. These are the pleasures which can't be accumulated, the luxury of the poor, the wonder of the professional survivor, he who is happy just to be on earth, content that he has been allowed to live there, and, further, that it has even pretended to accept him.

That's really all that traveling serves, to make more of this possibility of an un-relatable happiness: randomly taking a train and verifying that it leaves on time; to mentally succeed in one, two, or three sequences, as in gymnastics or dance; to remain the same in a landscape which doesn't remain, accompanying fragments of events, durations, pursuals, bodies happily reduced to their sex. Of course there's a heavy price to pay: obsessive set-backs, poor sequences of events, losses without profits, miserable failures and all the torment they bring to the table, which is derision itself.

This happiness is clandestine, just as the passion for cinema was for me semi-clandestine. It's my homosexual destiny, the man of the crowd, the roaming Jewish flirt, who only has his body with him, and only his body to obey him, a body he doesn't wash, that he treats without regard, as a friendly machine, destined to walk and to tire itself, to fill itself up and empty itself, to fuck, and ultimately it will be the first to cry uncle. In this sense I'm not a hedonist, because I distrust people who recount their pleasures technically, or, even worse, who make a war machine or an ideological display out of their cult of pleasure. I don't believe it, or I see in it a sort of vulgarity that comes from the class which isn't mine. On the other hand, nothing touches me more than the continually defeated, discouraged, and unwound obstinacy with which each of us tries to find a little bit of happiness on earth.

As for me, the *carelessness* with which I led my life is completely unbelievable. I never planned anything, had nothing programmed, or desired anything beyond the threshold of one or two months. Never. The questions that haunt a normal life simply didn't exist for me: to "earn" a living, to move up the social ladder, get married, have children, own things, to live with someone, to drive a car, all of that was resolved in the negative before having even been posed—since my mother never interfered in my life, there was no one to answer to. The only decision that I made in my life was when I left *Cahiers*. I said to myself: I can't do it any more, I'm stopping, and too bad about the consequences. The only decisions I ever made in my life were negative, like quitting my job at *Libération* a few years later. There is only one positive decision and it is an "End of the line, every one off" sort of decision, and that's *Trafic*. But ultimately I am very proud to have discovered that I was capable of a *positive* act.

I always knew your taste for postcards, but before the postcards, before the writing, there are the images and colors of the countries. That connects with today's idea that all of cinema is easily localizable, with the countries where cinema continues to exist, for better or for worse, and those where it has disappeared. And we have the technological means to summon this entire filmic memory.

The map, or the postcard comes before the territory. The map comes before the cinematographic image. The map is first. We should rather use the word from my childhood: atlas, the "little atlas," because we didn't have enough to buy a big one. Likewise the dictionary comes first, it is the preemptive law over all other books, the sole and true holy writing which recounts what took place and shows what existed. The egalitarian format of successive little images in the *Petit Larousse*[8] brings me back to the egalitarianism of high school. Many called, and certainly only a few chosen, but a single format for all the reels. It is as if parallel to the cult of "great men" there was a domain—iconography—where Napoleon didn't have the right to be fatter than his marshals. It's the same for the postcards.

I can't remember a time in my life when I didn't know with certainty that Tegucigalpa was the capital of Honduras or Windhoek that of old South West Africa. My good memory for proper names, foreign languages, and topography come from *one* image, a single image: the world made flat; and from an inextinguishable *jouissance*: the arbitrariness of the sign that occurs between the shape of Sweden and the word Sweden—there will always be a break there—and the fact that even in going to Sweden nothing will change. I was overjoyed when part of a map had an ambiguous status: was Sarre independent? I would have loved that, because one more country is a bonus. And what's the story with Dobroudja? So I took it upon myself to separate Dobroudja from Romania, from the color of Romania, and to maintain for myself the fiction of *one more* country whose capital would be Constantza.

It's to such feelings that I attribute the fact, maybe I'm exaggerating, that, denuded of all political ideology, I was as a child for an independent Algeria. I thought it wonderful that Algeria ceased to be the big pink thing for the French colonial empire, AOF, AEF.[9] I found it normal that the people should be the masters of their own home, but I also liked the idea of a new independent country. Perhaps it's this little word *independent* that counts. Independent as we all were in the family, very concerned with forbidding "degradation."

So there are the maps, I never stopped that. There's one at my house, the only image stuck to the wall, that of the IGN.[10] I am not at all an explorer or adventurer: I would never go to any country that didn't appear on a map. Deleuze said to me: You go to the end of the world to verify that the end of the world exists.[11] One goes to verify the immateriality of the border and the arbitrariness of the sign and one goes to infinitely enjoy the moment of coalescence that one approaches by plane when the map *is* the territory, and further that the two, like me, have a name!

The atlas is to the territory what the dictionary is to language, and you make the same domestic use of both of them: a means of reference.

The dictionary is like the sky, with as many stars as names, a good memory for the names, above all the foreign names, and the faces that have the right to appear there. *To end up* in the dictionary is an unavowed dream. And in the act of waiting comes this infinite promise of knowledge of a complicity with the works and the emotions. An entire life to have known that Alarcon wrote *The Suspicious Truth* without ever reading it, or to have known that Thorvaldsen or Canova are important sculptors without having ever verified it with my own eyes. A Platonic love with the starry sky.

It's certainly about seeing before naming.

Always. The name comes first. The thing we see is the name. It has to be verified that something responds "present" to this name. All cinephiles have a vice: that of lists. If I make a list, I exonerate myself of the fact that I don't appear there, or even that I spent my childhood afraid of not *being* on the list. Everything had to respond to its name—countries, cities, peoples, works—and we would have to be able to go and verify it. That's the way life goes and you ultimately finds yourself very ignorant, with the exception that, beyond a certain threshold, you're no longer questioned about your knowledge, about the concrete reality of this knowledge, about the bluff and bravado, about the madness it represents, or, in any case, about the desire to maintain a *personal*, intimate, relationship with all the pieces in the imaginary museum. Like a guard who will also *live* with what he protects, and with *that which protects him*.

This idea of lists is typical of the obsessive, always running the risk that a name, or a film, is missing on the roster.

It's for precisely that reason that I began my prologue with "Among the many films I've never seen ...," as a way of spilling the beans with bravado. What beans? The non-serious, that which as soon as there is a title and a film responds to it we will somehow end up—it's one of life's little ironies—seeing it. After all, the film I referenced the most today, *Night of the Hunter*, I saw and chose rather late.

Coming back to the postcards, there is always this idea of seizing the use value, of having it serve as a means of sending little coded messages to friends, signs that mean: I was there, I thought of you, that's what I have to say here and now. *There's a form of dandyism hidden behind the desire to have one's friends participate in an experience.*

The postcard was the only possible image for me after the map. I sent them to everybody, according to my loves, friendships, and fidelities. I ended up understanding that I was only sending them to myself, via my mother, who from my first trip got used to being "reassured" by a postcard. She ended up becoming the PO box for a pretty autistic cinema that I made with bits of cardboard, colorful stamps, and that maternal address that didn't change in over thirty years. One day, having a very confused understanding of the chronological *unfolding* of my life, I realized that the only line I could lay out to establish my trajectory year by year was the some fifteen hundred postcards I sent to my mother, which she was accustomed to conspicuously leave on a piece of furniture, so that upon returning I would find them and right away put them with the others. These days I'm saddened by the fact that the postcard—like cinema—is receding. Lately I've been going to Lyons, and as soon as I get off at Perrache I try to find postcards to send. But there is this enormous LYONS written on all of them, hideous frames, creative trinkets that are "chic and cheap," and I realize that *my* postcard, the one that I love, the aerial view, the cathedral or the marketplace, without anything written on it, no longer exists. What no longer exists is the imaginary extraction of a piece of landscape which becomes an image, an image which "flakes off," which comes near me, falls at my feet, on the stationary-store counter, and at the *tabac*. This image shouldn't have been written, signed, initialed, or stamped; it should be a dead leaf from an anonymous landscape. This is nevertheless what happens: just as there is a "filmed-cinema," over-signed, and over-signified, there is also a "posted-postcard" which deprives me of the fantasy that made me run in every direction, my entire life, behind the collection of snapshots that is the proof of my existence.

With the postcard there is a kind of bragging: on the one hand, there is the "I'm here, you're not, but we're still friends"; on the other hand, "At the end of the world I exist," "I'm in Shanghai as if I always lived here." And with the postcard there is something else that is ultimately rather political, which is that it's the product of a modest and anonymous commercial production that doesn't aim in any way towards art. The image of the world comes from the poorest, most destroyed people and their capacity to produce in their studios official and naïve images of their cities and countryside. Quite honestly, the photograph has been for me the *bad object* ideal. I tried, all the same, to take them myself, but that made me so anxious that I missed even the easiest of shots. It took being at *Libération* and working with Françoise Huguier, then Depardon, Peress, Lambours, or Vink, to see real photographers at work, and only then did I begin to have respect for this particularly phobic object of mine: the photograph. It's always the same story, that of *Kapo*, the feeling of *taking* a photograph, it is above all "taking," stealing, extorting, what for the most part—just look at photojournalism—remains true. I used to be rather iconoclastic about all this, and even at *Cahiers* I treated film stills pretty casually.

During the period of leftism, the disgust before photographic predation was almost itself reason enough to hate it. In India at the end of 1968 I was on the platform of a lousy train station waiting for a train and I was ready to kill people if they took pictures of the beggars. I was already skinny, jaundiced, with long hair and a beautiful local *kurta*: very believably an Indian and soon to be a beggar myself. There were two French tourists, a couple of bloats talking loudly whom I immediately hated. There was a little shoeshine boy whom they wanted to photograph and I purposely put myself in front of them, with an exalted air, so that they couldn't take the picture. I remember how they finally gave up exasperated, saying, "I can't take it because the tall guy is always in the way." The tall Indian was me and I was thrilled. I didn't want this kid ending up in a photo album. The truth is I wanted him for me.

We don't take pictures of the poor, and add our gaze or its aesthetic effects, we go to *them* and we buy their photos and their postcards from them, helping—in however little a way—the local artisanal market—and we send them to our friends as signs of life, as messages in bottles. Sometimes it's difficult because we're not in a postcard culture, like India for instance. I was very moved to find the same card of old Delhi, a little flimsy and blurry, ten years later, and to send it a second time. I imagined the modest, indifferent persistence of the studio that continued to print that little image. Finally the postcard is ideal for coded messages or for signifying to another that we'd like them to enter into such and such a complicity. That's the *perverse* aspect of the postcard: it has to be able to be read by both the mailman and its recipient, and each of them has to understand something different. It had to be that the images mysteriously came from the real itself, normal and without fuss, and become the place itself of a *private* communication. At the same time it's the respect for the real across the most visible of its images and the opacification for me—for "us"—of this false visibility for everyone. This sleight of hand always enchanted me and I continue to practice it until the end, knowing full well its cause. It's also what pushed me towards the cinema—popular cinema.

It's the metaphor for cinema: everything can be seen by everyone, except that those who so desire can find even more to see. What's interesting, beginning there, is how to create a matrix, not political but affective, ideological and moral, where the images from below will resist this coded language, this visual imposed or withheld by the West.

The most beautiful postcards are obviously those in which the beauty seems neither planned nor willed by someone. I say "seems" because I could almost, and it's truly a perverse idea, reconstruct a *politique des auteurs* staring with the different types of shots, styles of framing, and the main postcard producers. Isn't this what we agreed to do with American cinema?

Where I almost stumbled into catastrophe was when the postcard, this strange *clandestine* umbilical chord, couldn't be found. Why travel if I didn't encounter any images on my path? One year I spent a week in Trinidad because I was intrigued by it. A sinister week where I hated the hotel, rigorously spoke to no one, and roamed around in a bad mood. A trip that only I could take. First thing, upon arrival: where are the postcards? I can't find them. I almost said, "I'm leaving, my collection is ruined, it's not going to have the words Port-of-Spain, the link Trinidad-and-Tobago." And then, in a big drugstore run by Indians with a crumpled air, I found a little pile of cards in bulk and I immediately snatched them up, more than satisfied. From that

moment on I *began* to see Port-of-Spain. Sometimes I would even start by looking at the postcard instead of where I was, before confronting its model! I believe people like me do everything backwards: they begin by *seeing language* and then later, little by little, they begin *speaking images*. There is a certain way of "becoming one" with cinema which tinkers with itself like that right from the start.

The postcard isn't a spontaneous shot; it offers an anonymous mise-en-scène, *and a standard point of view. Your pleasure consists of playing with this pre-*mise-en-scène, *of making it ironic, or being in the shot.*

I always prefer the general view of the city. There are images of Tokyo taken from the big hotels in Shinjuku that give me as much pleasure as the actual view itself.

Today we have passed from the postcard-image to imagery.

I think I detest imagery. There were never many images in my home during childhood. Those of the two familiar dictionaries—the medical (blue), and the culinary (red)—equally terrifying and which smelled like ink, those contemptuous images from catechism, those of sports magazines, sepia, green, blue, for a while during the Tour de France, those of *Tintin* which for a period I devoured, being in love with cinema without knowing it—the art of linking—which was already the driving force of Hergé and above all Jacobs.[12] But never any taste for the *beautiful images*.

It would be good to start from the beginning: so when was your love of cinema born?

I went to the cinema very early. The theater was just below on the corner. There were a lot of theaters in the neighborhood, all of which have disappeared: Cinéphone Saint-Antoine, Cyrano-Roquette, Gaumont-Voltaire, Lux-Bastille, Royal Variétés, Magic, Artistic-Voltaire. My mother and aunt love the cinema, and I remember how wonderful it was to "decide at the last minute" to put off the dishes and homework until later, and suddenly find ourselves on the sidewalk, uncertain as to what film we would see, nearly missing the only screening at 9 o'clock at night, with its procession of *in vivo* horrors—the "attractions" that I spoke of in *La Rampe*.

The cinema was above all *natural*. I saw films. I loved it. I don't believe that it could have marked me more than any other kid of that era. Because of me my mother had to see a lot of Italian "cloak-and-sword" films. As for me I had to see a lot of melodramas, which were also Italian. The doxa of the house was: Italian films are beautiful, but sad, but we loved this totally contrived sadness.

The true birth at the cinema, and it isn't at all banal, is almost conscious. It was the junction between the legend of the father and the first confrontation in the 1950s with the images of the reality of the camps. The image which ultimately held the right of preemption over all others. My cinephilia had been *programmed* and the consciousness that I had of it was relayed clearly by the yellow period *Cahiers*, and by Henri Agel. Not necessarily the "when you love life, you go to the cinema"[14] kind, which to this day seems to me both tacky and false. Nevertheless, a drug stronger than any other.

Ultimately it shouldn't be forgotten that this programming was done with sound, with the voice. I was told that my father was in "post-synch," a word that I always knew. His body was one thing, and his voice another: it was very strange. Well before television there was the radio, and I believe that my culture is at base that of the radio of the 1950s, with *Le Grenier de Montmartre, Le Passe-temps des dames et demoiselles*, the *route du Tour*, Monsieur Champagne, Zappy Max, *Signé Furax*, and the Omo theater.

It's the voice that counts, which recounts, which says that this took place, that we saw a film and it showed *X*. During Sunday brunch my mother would tell my grandmother about the film she and I had seen that week. I thought she told it sublimely. The pleasure of listening to her was as great as seeing the film for a second time.

The image is already doubled by commentary, or an echo: something we can almost call, in a sense, critical.

Cinema isn't a technique of displaying images, it's an *art of showing*, and showing is a gesture, a gesture that demands looking and watching. Without this gesture there is just imagery. But if something is shown, someone *must* acknowledge its receipt. There were certainly other ways of spending one's life with cinema, but this is how I spent mine. It's very tennis-like, this idea that it would be scandalous not to *return* a serve. I was never a great server, but I believe that, like Jimmy Connors, I was good at returning.

How do we reconcile two rather contradictory propositions, at least in appearance: the cinema would promise a world (why not a better one?), and the first images, the original images, would be those of the camps? Doesn't that determine a kind of moral trajectory? For others, couldn't this relationship to cinema be born across a different configuration?

The promise of a world that begins with a catastrophe isn't necessarily contradictory. Sometimes I think that my generation is the only one to have found in its heritage unacceptable, abject racism disqualified for ever. In a way that created so absolutely, through its repercussions, a kind of euphoria of mourning, as well as a certain candid propensity for a *tabula rasa*, as in, "OK, the worst took place, it's enough to never forget it and it will never happen again."

Most filmmakers whom you defend never stop recalling it, particularly the Straubs.

Of course. Those who make up the New Wave are only about fifteen years older than I am. As children they were exposed to something similar. For the Straubs it's their whole life, it's what they do. Remembering that on the one hand it mustn't be forgotten, and on the other it mustn't be rebuilt. Because at this point everything is written in a kind of palimpsest which maintains the traces, the evidence, the scars, and the accents: that which "makes believe." I encountered the Straubs every time the theme of *resistance* crossed my life. Like hitting your heels against the bottom of the sea before coming back up to the surface, where you can breathe. At the same time, this assimilation of cinema with the idea of "resistance" is strange.

There is a whole period of French cinema just prior to the New Wave that you feel very distant from. Why this aversion?

I did my best to sneak past it, but before becoming a professional cinephile I over-*identified* myself with the bodies and voices of French actors. My grandmother, who always valorized ugly men, had the habit of recalling (in speaking of Michel Simon, who was still alive, or of Harry Baur, who was dead and whom I didn't discover until much later in the films of Maurice Tourneur, who had been "aribor"[15] for me) to what extent these fat and slightly monstrous (and for the record not very seductive) actors were also exceptional actors. All true by the way, but I wonder if perhaps I didn't make the connection between their ugliness and their talent, as if one naturally went with the other. Ugliness being the shameless theme of many of Fernandel's films for instance. Today I could say it like this: French actors are great actors but they are sexually implausible. Not long ago I was watching Becker's *Rue de l'Estrapade* on cable. I don't know Becker well and I'm a little ashamed of it, as he had to be the *only* filmmaker who, at the time of my moving out of early childhood, loved the young French actors of the day, young men like Daniel Gélin and Louis Jourdan, and young women like Anne Vernon, who were just the right age to be the first young post-war stars. Oh well, it didn't happen. I don't know what happened, but ten years later, before the New Wave, the recurring faces of French cinema were again the *holy monsters* from between the wars: Fernandel, Gabin, Fresnay, Brasseur, Noël-Noël. As a result the French cinema was offering a French kid like me his *grandparents*, grandpas and grandmas; they were terrific, but rather bitter and anti-youth. You had to love the way in which they didn't love us! Recently watching one of the big films from that time, *L'Homme aux clés d'or*, I was astounded by the hate oozing from it, all in the glory of an aging Fresnay, and where the young are all portrayed as the abject sons of spineless fathers. So what became of the Gelins, Auclairs, Pellegrins, Periers, and *tutti quanti*? They didn't fit the bill, they were second string, in theater, or something else. They were replaced by their parents. It's impossible for me not to see in this the prolongation of Vichy, the trickery of a generation, the persistence of an old France, deafly disqualified, to such an extent that the New

Wave wouldn't have to immediately overturn the language of cinema: the sole fact of using actors *their own age*, Bardot and Belmondo, sufficed to explode it.

How could a 10-year-old child, unless he was a "bad" child, identify with Michel Simon—who was ugly but terrific? Of course there was the ex-sex bomb Gabin with his graying temples, but for me he was almost the anti-erotic figure *par excellence*, and I only liked him in two or three roles: *Gueule d'amour* and *Le Plaisir*.

I have to admit that there was nothing for me in that French herd; nothing to mark out the desire. Of the names at the top of the posters, I preferred such and such a second role, always on the side of the *losers*. But with Gérard Phillipe, I heard the creaking of the floorboards, the voice of a skinny little twit, and I absolutely knew that in the Franco-American arm-wrestle, we were off to a bad start, and there was almost a feeling of shame in being from the same country as *Fanfan la Tulipe* once you saw *Scaramouche*. This vague, indignant feeling I had about my country comes back to me now very strongly. The moment Paul Touvier was acquitted, I don't think I exaggerate, there would forever be something *irreconcilable*.[16]

That's why very consciously becoming a cinephile was to identify with *something else*. The fact that there was someone *behind* the camera, that this someone could be a man, an auteur, and in the final analysis a father. That allowed me to avoid the question of the actor, as if it had been decided once and for all. And decided it was. It was enough just to watch Cary Grant, James Stewart, Robert Ryan, and Henry Fonda in the 1950s, with their graying temples, to know that's where the charm was, that the seduction, the desire to be kidnapped, was there. We still experience this among cinephiles: we talk about the actors we like, the ones we don't like, we speak about the French, and then we speak about the Americans, and from there we never stop. I can say that, mythologically, my cinematic parents are not French. The father is American, and I'm with him as the little John Mohune is in the cinephilic myth incarnated in the film *Moonfleet*: "The exercise was beneficial, sir."[17] For women it is the opposite: the desirable woman, she who remained "natural," who is neither dyed, lifted, nor continuously smiling from ear to ear like the talking heads at CNN, she is the big Italian sister, Mangano, Bosé, Podesta, and later

Cardinale. That said, we have to believe that I immediately had an execrable taste for feminine beauty since I thought Gianna Maria Canale, who is in fact an overweight cow, was the stone-cold beauty incarnate!

This French impasse, that of the actor's body, in a certain way explains how the specificity of French cinema rests on a moral, rather than physical, presence.

Yes. To preach is to lecture, to teach someone a lesson. As if France was punished precisely for that. I was never expecting a "great show" from my country, and those from my childhood—Guitry for example—already seemed to be worm-eaten.

You often come back to the Rivette article on Gillo Pontecorvo's Kapo, *a film that you confess you've never seen. What is it that you found so appealing about this article? The rhetorical dimension? The fact that someone allowed himself to write in a journal that it is forbidden to do a track forward onto barbed wire?*

Cahiers was the journal that dedicated three frivolous lines at the end of an issue to a film that the whole world was whistling the song from, David Lean's *The Bridge on the River Kwai*! Either they were imposters and snobs, or they had an idea, their own rationale, other values. They didn't take public taste into consideration. They didn't even respect Fritz Lang's opinion when he claimed openly that he didn't like his own Indian diptych![18] In other words, the film had to be sufficient for them, there had to be a *truth* of film that wasn't the condition of production, its context, or its success at the box office; a truth which authorized speaking up and which inspired these people to make this extraordinary object that was the yellow period *Cahiers*. That must have confirmed for me that *Cahiers* was "my place," above all the day someone dared to pronounce this verdict with the vehemence of Péguy,[19] which I shared hands down. Except that Rivette's verdict bore the question of the tracking shot as well as that of *framing*. I adhered to this easily, only because the frame was already my natural language, the only one where I felt at ease. I could follow the adventures of the frame effortlessly with Hitchcock, Lang, Mizoguchi, or Preminger. The exacerbated, erotic, consciousness of what's inside and what's outside, of what enters, what leaves, and finally the very original status of this "outside," the *out of frame* of cinema, which ten years later the people at *Cahiers* would create theoretical orgies out of. But I was less at ease with the filmmakers who didn't appear to draw their effects from this eroticization of the frame. I had trouble with Rossellini and Walsh, and I was a little ashamed because these were the auteurs of *Cahiers*. I didn't find my reference points. The temple columns were for me—a scrawny Samson—the frame as a living cut-out, a scalpel-eye, a surgical rectangle, etc. I liked this cruelty, but I hadn't yet seen its reverse: compassion. Mizoguchi, "Mizo" as we said, was my favorite filmmaker.

I ended up no longer being a slave to the frame, the cut. I began to find beauty in films which derived their energy from the *middle* of the image, which put important things in the center so that we could clearly see them. Walsh, of course, and above all Ford. After that the question receded, because the filmmakers of the frame weren't as good, and, beginning with Rossellini, the best of modern cinema was made in *precipitation* of the shot, in an optical short-circuit across spaces which had nothing to do with the moral of the frame or the tracking shot. That is why Rivette's demonstration, absolutely true at the time, would have to be reformulated in light of contemporary cinema.

The basis of this story, if I dare say, is my *reconciliation* with cinema. The frame is the cruelty, the obligation not to flee, and not to shy away from what *is*, and the cinema alone was able to tame it. But today this cruelty doesn't seem all that terrible. On the contrary I find in it a human dimension, even humanist, that risks decline in the future. The cinema has this capacity—Bazin's fantasy—to cut the skin from images, from reality itself–and that hurts–but it also has the capacity to atone for what was thus framed, extracted, and put into light. I have the sense of going from one extreme to the other of a single question: the question of light. The light which accuses and the light which saves. This is why I was recently thinking that the most ancient arts—literature, painting—have maintained a violence which is essentially lacking in the cinema.

Is there not also the fact that we are in a sense done with the cinema of intimidation or terror, and that we want to move on to something else?

The cinema of terror that we knew and supported produced what needed to be produced. That must have ended around 1975, with the death of Pasolini. Later on it will have to be determined how the intimidation of the 1970s will be rediscovered in the 1990s. It's still too soon to tell. As for myself, I feel a little calmer, a little more open, but there is also going to be something of the age that no longer imagines the bitter and sincere passions we have experienced.

All that's left for me is to become—along the lines of Godard—a sort of lawyer for the won cause of cinema. I say only that cinema was a big deal, much bigger than we believed, even if today it's smaller than we believe. And I speak of cinema as a friend, as a being with whom I spent my life. Today it is tempting to think that we grew old together and that we're almost going to die together. The cinema of terror is behind us. Contemporary cinema—with its many good films—is more a meticulous exploration of the mental *case* (in the sense of Oliveira's film *My Case*). Still, I don't see any return to the ludic values of yesterday—the small films adored in spite of the entire "Saturday night" cinema. Today the wager of images passes by the violence of media and advertising, a violence which from now on cinema seems to be exempted from. The strategy of Benetton, reality shows, the Gulf War without images, those are serious things today, things I take seriously. But ultimately I am more like a slightly out-of-step observer, a citizen, a *belle âme*. More than twenty years ago I had this idea that the commercial was the Trojan horse of something that would soon reveal its face. It was entitled "Sur Salador."[20]

If we could go back chronologically to the story, particularly of the 1960s, I'd like it if you would tell me about the famous trip with Louis Skorecki to Hollywood in 1964, when you decided to visit a number of illustrious and aging auteurs: was it a way for you to buy your way into Cahiers du cinéma, *by turning in a few big interviews with the last of the Hollywood pioneers?*

I have no idea what I was doing at that time, nor what I was thinking, what I planned *a fortiori*! It's clear that the trip was the initiative of Skorecki, who was back then very dynamic and someone I followed. I was following the crowd, the pretext being to become part of *Cahiers*. Or rather: to become *indispensable* to *Cahiers*, of which we were already on the path—in order to be there for good, a little more than just tolerated. Antoine de Baecque's book[21] allowed me to understand the imbroglio of the time a little better, perhaps the only moment of crisis and of choice in the history of the journal. Skorecki and I were still very much on the side of Douchet, the MacMahonians,[22] classic cinema, etc. But Rivette needed someone to take over in order to move on to something else, to a post-Rohmer. I'm forced to re-create that from the exterior because it's all a foggy memory, a cloud that prevents me from seeing *how* I got through—if it was more the desire of L.S., C.D.,[23] or my own?—this "entry into *Cahiers*" which seemed inescapable at the time and was spent in a sort of bad mood. In any case, the 1960s, whose generous insouciance is today shocking, were for me somnambular years in which I have the sense that I never existed. I use dates to scan desperately for something: if 1968 is the moment of awakening, 1964 is that of the trip to America and my first published articles in *Cahiers*: my name in the yellow *Cahiers, in extremis*, four issues before changing the formula! Ultimately it has to be said that we didn't write just like that, point blank, that you were supposed to have seen many films before authorizing yourself to write. It's five years between the shock of *Hiroshima* and my article on Tashlin's *Who's Minding the Store?*[24] It seemed natural because there was still this idea—untenable today—that you could "recapture" the films of the past, to again feel—*in extremis*—that we were their slightly lagging contemporaries. The idea of "classics," and of repertoire, left us indifferent: it was enough that an authorized speech told us that Feuillade or Dovzhenko were good in order to be torn from the past and plunged into our present.

The trip to America was of the same belief that what is valuable is necessarily of the "present." I never abandoned this belief: what is no longer *active* can be left to the sociologists, culturologists, and the erudite; it doesn't concern me at all. But obviously, as a result you're unable to see that all you've collected is a series of touching *nevermores*.

I don't think that, in front of Keaton, Renoir, McCarey, or Sternberg, I thought for a moment that they were going to die, or that we would never see them again. Which was nevertheless totally obvious. L.S., myself, and our little group were in fact gerontophiles at the time: we were thrilled with the late works of the great masters like Titian's last drawings, the solitude purged of style, the boldness in the midst of a certain obsolescence, a certain way of approaching a pure logic of cinema—and only cinema. *The 1,000 Eyes of Dr. Mabuse*, *Gertrud*, *Seven Women*, like *Anatahan* or *A King in New York*, are the films of old-timers, exposed to the condescendence of official criticism, running to their aid ready to fight for them. And the fact that even if today—given my age—I admit that there is often something essential in the first works of an auteur, I am still moved by the films of the old-timers: Kurosawa, Oliveira, Buñuel. At both ends of the chain, between the carelessness of a spoiled energy and the economy of a time that one can't afford to waste, there is the beauty of cinema, this art where the physical state of those who make it is so clear.

Arriving *in extremis*, almost too late, pretending to believe that the banquet is still taking place, is without a doubt the essence of what we call cinephilia. The cinephile isn't *nostalgic* for a golden age that he did or didn't know, and of which he thinks there has been no equal since. Rather, the cinephile is the one who, watching a film that has just been released, a contemporary film, already feels the passing, the "that will have been." You feel it in an agonizing way, for instance in the films of Demy, beginning with *Lola*. So, it's possible that this melancholy, by dint of being the common denominator of all films, has for me blurred the difference between those of the past and those of the present. Inversely, the nostalgic continues wanting to know how it was better before, even if it means offering himself a private spectacle or even a museum-like reconstitution. I always react rather poorly when someone speaks to me of "nostalgia"; like all melancholics, I have a taste for the present itself, like journalism, which thinks one day after another. The present for me is a sort of absolute resistance, a defiance of the necessity of planning, programming, and previewing, and above all of working personally to obtain one's pleasures: that which exasperates and horrifies me. Actually, the present is the luxury of he who has nothing, nothing but his non-accumulated pleasures, which are the consciousness of the dawning of a new day, of the sun on one's skin, a café terrace, and the passing by of others; it is the pride of those who possess nothing, and it is already the tracking shot in *Kapo*: you can't have both the action of the scene *and* the camera movement, you have to choose. No accumulation, no administration, this word that has known so much success, the obligation to be in the way of things, as they come, one by one, towards me and the only body I have and to which something will have to be "returned"—orally, written, or oral writing. The perfusion of the present.

Does the stoic idea hold any value for you? A certain manner of resisting, a proud affront to the present?

I have this strange sort of "exchange of friendly services" and probably a little sleight of hand between two value systems. Nevertheless, concerning what is mine, my fate, my destiny—I always believed that everyone had a destiny, so why not me?—I oppose a certain contempt, a *fin de non-recevoir.*[25] You don't fight against common fate, you accept illness and death, but in return you don't talk about them. The proximity of death doesn't play the role, as I believed as a young critic, of a "surplus meaning," but is only the exacerbation of a desire for meaning that existed before. There is no last word, and in the final analysis, one is reasonably *duped.* There is a sort of objective absurdity in seeing the *image* that's going to replace you being put into place, that which is going to cover over all the others—and in my case, against which I work quickly, with my back against the wall: a sort of 'cine-tombstone' for a nice guru of cinephilia. On the other hand, for the others, the injustices, the politics, the winners and the losers, it is nevertheless the old Promethean myth that will function until the end. It is this pride of the foundling that says the only cause he will not embrace is his own, because it is profoundly crude to complain. Because that would be admitting that one has done me wrong. I admire—without really liking—those who have the fortitude to conduct trials against their own countries, like Syberberg and Thomas Bernhard. They have found enemies of their own caliber. I could consider myself a victim, a victim of a war, for instance, but I looked hard and couldn't find anyone to blame.

You didn't answer my question about the trip to America.

Alright, America. In 1964 I was 20, and there were still a few sublime old-timers in Los Angeles. For instance Leo McCarey, who had never done an interview, neither at *Cahiers*, nor anywhere else, so we were the first. McCarey wasn't a sublime old-timer, he was a sick man, an extremely emaciated (compared to the pictures) has-been, and also very bitter. L. and I experienced the interview, which took place in the cafeteria of I don't remember what big studio, as perfectly "McCareyian," as proof of a well founded *politique des auteurs*. It was pure awkwardness. McCarey was eating yogurt and spilling it all over the place, while singing the praises of his first film in a somewhat sour voice. We saw his senility. Naturally we also found it atrocious that the 1940s box office smash was twenty years later this survivor. It seemed like we experienced the cruelty of Hollywood, of the system, and we knew which side we were on.

We didn't go there to find just anyone. We had a list of those whom we wanted to see and many of them were going into exile or disappearing. Those in charge of the "foreign press," seeing us ask to speak with Jacques Tourneur, must have taken us for nuts, but they handled it rather well, as they very matter-of-factly called Tourneur from his seat at the Directors' Guild. We saw a tall man arrive, a little hesitant, who spoke to us immediately in a southern French accent. Occasionally we would stumble upon more contemporary filmmakers, those who were more conscious of their situation: Sam Fuller, who was delighted to play the role that wasn't quite yet his in front of two European kids, or Jerry Lewis, who, in the middle of shoot with Tashlin, interrupted the scene to show everyone the special issue of *Cahiers* where he had ranked among the *filmmakers*!

On the other hand, I remember the way Cukor treated us as what we must have been and appeared to be from the outside: a couple of crackpot amateurs, one fat, one skinny, full of admiration and determined not to be disappointed. I often think about this episode with Cukor as you might think about some episode that you couldn't see at the time to what extent it was emblematic. It was a hot summer day in an amazing villa, among his courtiers and minions, and everyone there seemed to be blossoming, except for us, drenched in sweat, saying how much we loved *Sylvia Scarlett*, which we just discovered in Paris. Cukor wasn't particularly flattered that we valorized one of his flops from the beginning of his career. Just like Katharine Hepburn in her autobiography, excusing herself for having made it, and immediately lowering herself in my esteem. The law of showbiz is that a commercial failure *can't be* a good film. When I imagine the two of us with that old broken man, crafty as a monkey, and whose last film *Rich and Famous* proved that he never went senile, I am still astounded by the way we chose to love American cinema not by their norms but by our own.

At some point the conversation touched upon Nicholas Ray, and we must have said that we loved *Wind across the Everglades*. Hearing this, Cukor started howling, the laugh of a mean and sour old lady, crying to the others, "Come here, come here! You know which film they like? *Wind across the Everglades*! The film that Jack Warner didn't even dare release!" I can still see us irritated but unshaken, persuaded that we were right, and in fact we were. It was just like six years later when for our first course at Censier, Pascal Bonitzer and myself, mortified at the front of the red lecture hall—coming unstitched, and when interrogating the cinema oscillating between Sam Peckinpah and Francesco Rosi—howled in blanching voices that materialist cinema was Godard and Gorin's *Vent d'Est* and the Straubs' *Not Reconciled*, and there was to be no compromise. This feeling of remaining a sincere and stubborn child with all his caprices in the face of the condescending and bloated good sense of the adult world is certainly something that I'm still a little proud of.

The cinephile isn't the one who loves and copies in life the objects and attitudes that he first loved on the screen. He is at the same time both more modest and infinitely prouder: what he asks of cinema is to *endure* like cinema. He might need the *politique des auteurs*, but in the sense that a film obeys a point of view, a vision of the world that legitimizes it, gives it its logic. But ultimately the film becomes a sort of being, a character, a kind of portrait of Dorian Gray in which I can see myself aging. That's why we didn't make too much of Cukor turning his nose up at *Sylvia Scarlett*. It's why I've always had a little bit of pity for the madmen of American cinema—the sweet fetishists—who spent their lives disguising themselves as little Americans of the 1950s, with their boots, jackets, and cars. This explains how I was able to learn to breathe outside polluted France in American cinema, and at the same time I had no problem being furious in the 1970s with American imperialism.

Intellectually, America was completely at peace: it was a very powerful world that never stopped demanding of us, and secreting in itself antibodies of lucidity, irony, and cracks. France was an oversized midget, and America was a giant which could produce internal dissidents who were our heroes: from Welles to Ray, the martyrologue was inexhaustible and the most "normal" thing in the world. This astounding split, this American presence at the heart of my culture and nowhere in my dreams, is perhaps difficult to understand today; as difficult as the "communist dream," which was its parallel. The falling aesthetics of Yalta have finished falling.

What do you think of this assumption that cinema is finished with the national idea? In effect, except for a few rather rare cases, Hollywood, France, India, and maybe Hong Kong and Egypt, cinema is no longer conflated with the geographic territories, but has become a small country of its own, minor in the vast world of images, but a country nonetheless where everyone knows each other. The country of cinema is that of festivals, which allows Jim Jarmusch to be close to Emir Kusturica, though they have nothing in common culturally. The question is what becomes of the promise of the world with a cinema whose territory has singularly shrunk?

Godard was the first to assimilate the Cinema with a country, one more country on a map. Obviously, I like this idea very much and I take it up. Cinema is the country that is missing from my map. We now wonder if it is an empire, a nation, or a province. It was an empire when there were still empires. When I was a kid we never saw Russian films, but we loved them anyway, preemptively. In fact, we knew that the Soviets made a lot of films and we thought that was good. Even the English carried on for a while.

Even when Godard developed those beautiful and simple metaphors with Hollywood-Mosfilm,[26] it was already over. Nothing was more comic—and without a doubt "human"—than the way we were afraid of things which haven't been frightening for a long time.

It seems that each generation was "always ready" to just solve the problems of their predecessors. It's the famous "late war." As for the current situation in the country of Cinema, it isn't vital enough to produce anything comparable to the past. There was an empire, certainly, but it allowed Ambassador Eisenstein to play tennis with Chaplin. There was a world war, but that allowed Buñuel and Ivens, sitting around Hollywood, to write a script for Garbo. Closer to us, when Fassbinder remade Sirk, when Godard spoke with Lang, or Glauber Rocha gave hell to Pasolini *post mortem*, there was a country because it had true inhabitants who spoke the same language. That was the beauty of the "new cinemas" of the 1960s, and it too evaporated. The best contemporary filmmakers are not really "brothers"; they are confronted more by the withering of their margins of maneuverability which make them look like each other, not like brothers, not even like rivals. That only exists at the festivals. Cannes, for instance, goes to a lot of trouble to invent—by means of the Palme d'Or—a presentable American independent cinema. That creates a style, the global style of "quality films," the "cinephilic" style, and that would explain the unanimity of current criticism, unable to do anything other than mimic disagreement. At the same time that helps me understand to what extent the promise of the world wasn't for me the certainty of one day playing the part of an upper-crust cinephile (I was carefully kept outside of the official posts) but rather it was the dream of "without nations or borders," far away from nationalism.

Coming back to Cahiers *of the 1960s, what role did Jean Douchet play in your beginning to write about cinema?*

Jean was certainly the only one who gave us the green light and encouragement to write. In this sense his mediation was priceless. To write and be published was the only test of truth. The rest didn't exist, it was unimportant. *Cahiers* always kept the heads of those who wrote just above water. The clever, the ambitious, and the worldly never stayed long. Once I was at the Champs-Elysées,[27] I must have seen Rohmer from afar. It felt like being in a dentist's office for the rich, but you didn't want to be loved, you only wanted to be a part of *Cahiers*.

How did you position yourself in relation to the journal's influential struggles, for example with Douchet and Rivette, who didn't defend the same positions?

For me it's a good paradigm, because thirty years later I must be one of the rare few who feels comfortable with both of them. They are also the two faces of *my* personality. If back then I never imagined the struggles that took place at *Cahiers*, I did cook up theories for a long time, with a friend from school, about this impossible couple, each of them showing us the way from their respective sides. On the side of Rivette there were the short, categorical, tubercular texts, the "Letter on Rossellini," and the lively moral. With Douchet, there were the scholarly texts, spiraling, the dandyism of a great bourgeois lover of the arts, the crazy hermenaut who nevertheless introduced us to an attitude that followed us: it was right to *interpret*. Rivette taught me not to be afraid of seeing, and Douchet, not to be afraid of reading. My friend, very mystical, was more on Rivette's side, and I was on Douchet's. What's funny is that the two men opposed each other in every way. By the fact that Rivette discovered all those incredible people *avant la lettre*, he moved across criticism "film by film." Douchet, on the other hand, needs to think, to be certain, to have a *work* in front of him, and he had to wait until after 1960 for it—Garrel, for instance—to be made. One was at the very beginning of things, the other at the very end. Ultimately the difference was also sexual: Douchet was certainly looked down upon as a homosexual and is further the totally radiant kind. It seems to me that the New Wave remained decidedly homophobic. As for me, I belong to the tradition dominated by *Cahiers*, which ended up confusing love and friendship, and which was surprised that friendship wasn't even a bit more sublime.

Let's talk about May '68. What were you doing at the time and how did you see the ideological confusion? There is a question that seems to me to be important: how do you explain the fact that May '68 was an unfilmed event for French cinema? One has the sense that no script came out of it, as if the meeting between the cinema and reality would reveal itself as impossible.

I took the *événements* straight in the face, like a neighborhood wastrel who had nothing to lose, just do and think, and who was perhaps waiting for something—something apocalyptic: ripping and revelatory—to tear him from this lethargy. Afterwards, while writing about *Mourir à trente ans* for instance, I reflected on to what extent the cinema didn't take part in the events of '68. For me, at the time, it was worse: by their very nature the events *forced* us to abandon cinema, or rather turn our backs on it. I didn't find myself on the side of *Cahiers*, the "General Estates"[28] of cinema. I was part of a small group of vociferous anarcho-dandies for whom the revolutionary cinematic program was "poetry will be made by all." It was a small group of people, those from Rohmer's *La Collectioneuse*, gathered around Silvina Boissonas'[29] money, which a few of them wanted to use to move "behind the camera." Only one remains and he was the best: Phillipe Garrel. We must have formed a collective, as I see myself two steps away from my house filming the line in front of the chairman of Crédit Lyonnais between two piles of garbage. The bourgeois folks taking their money out of the bank trembling in the middle of this vileness, which made us very happy. It was Battaillean, and we read Battaille a lot—*The Story of the Eye* still covertly—during the cinematheque years. Between the return of the old flame of anarcho-syndicalism and the sorcerer's apprentice of radical chic, there were little provisional routes we could take. It was decided that everything filmed individually would be put into the collective pot for the great "film synthesis," and I see Garrel, young and fragile, saying, with total contempt, something like, "Yeah, OK, I'm not against the soup kitchen." The opacity of the cinematic image in 1968 is astonishing. The footage on TV is rarely more eloquent: we see young people with short hair and close-fitting suits, throwing cobble-stones, arguing for hours, but all *in astounding ignorance of their image!*

Parallel to that there was the theater. How did I find myself at Censier in that yellow classroom, preparing to take over the Odeon? I have no idea. There was a little group there as well, but I only remember Jean-Jacques Lebel, who was trying to be some kind of post-Renaud-Barrault or I don't know what. At the time I didn't speak in public; actually all my life, speaking in public deeply troubled me. However, I can see myself sitting on a radiator, countering Lebel in a faint voice, on the theme of "No, we won't even play Artaud. There will be no representation other than the one the people give themselves." That's what happened in the first days of the Odeon, and not without panache. The Terror. One night we stormed the theater, and I can see the bakery where I had to buy the cookies in case there was a siege. The place was empty and it was my strange "punishment" to camp out there for a little while, as I had always considered the theater as the opposite of "my place," as a place of unease. The only photo I have of myself from 1968 appeared in *Noir et blanc*: I'm in a suit, sitting cross-legged on the stage of the Odeon while Barrault and Renaud plead their cause. Velour pants, short hair, and already with a moustache.

That said, I was, and still am, particularly sensitive to the themes of the day, like "the society of the spectacle." I read Debord's book and even then advertising provoked in me a strange mix of ironic contempt and fear. I believe today that if I was the only one at *Cahiers* who never lost this thread, it's because it's mine, and coincidentally it's also a part of that of the time. It's because already advertising too effectively controlled *the ideal comedy* that I was angry at. Out of "true" idealism, of course. And this idealism, in 1968, was for me the *tabula rasa*, the adieu to the "suffocating" culture, and the discount selling of my only treasures (books and records: the complete works of Stevenson and Monteverdi's *Orpheus*). The theater was symbolically the good place, where one was finally done with representation. The cinema seemed wholly in the realm of alienation. One day in a little theater, there were these people who were very set on the fact that they had something to tell us like, "Now comrades, we're moving on to serious things, namely the armed struggle, for those who are not in agreement there's still time to leave." I was with a friend, and we looked at each other and split. A little man got up and said, "I respect your ideas, but my convictions prevent me from killing." Someone said that he had the right to his convictions and he left. I found all of that rather gallant, just like in books. In fact the man was Paul Virilio, and we brought this scene up twenty years later.

I was never really much on the side of *Cahiers*. I believe I was still seeing Louis Skorecki a lot. The first days of May 1968 remain enchanted for me, like someone who is disabled suddenly discovering that he can *naturally* be a part of the picture, part of the streets on which one strolled down the middle, the spontaneous discussions, the ludic game of tennis between action and reaction, part of a Paris more beautiful then ever, and, for me, with absolutely nothing in my hands, nothing in my pockets. There was my political candor, my immediate arrogance, the facility with which I identified with a cause, anti-authoritarian revolt, the student cause, which until that point had left me cold (for me the student was a shameful, Gombrowiczian being), and the possibility that I too could revel in big words, like the word "revolution" for instance.

My lack of political culture was unfathomable. It's why I spent one part of my life mixing up moral and aesthetic, and another part mixing up moral and political. What's certain is that I expected from this "revolution" the legitimacy it gave to my taste for *dispossession*, to my own ineptitude at planning, attaining goals, the promise of tomorrows, and to accumulating and *calculating* in general. The revolution was *hic et nunc*, more immanence in the life of more people, suddenly able to have a dialogue, something like that. It was the opposite of a prophesy, and moreover it resembled the promises of paradise, even on earth, and that awoke in me the disbelief of a child shocked by religion, which had to have recourse to such things. The idea of a better life always seemed worthless to me, and if I was never interested in religion, it's certainly not because of religious indifference, but rather that, living as I did in the cine-limbo of this world, I consider this to be the only world which exists, and which exists all the more so that I remained a prisoner to the fact that I never attained it. Cinephilia is this healthy illness of which one of the symptoms is that this world here is already another world.

This is why I always watch the phenomena of trance, hysteria, and mass belief incredulously: I almost always think they're *faking it*! On the other hand, I believe that everyone, in spite of their little cries about their fate and their gazes turned towards "a better life" (as Willem says), always touches *hic et nunc* the material and spiritual benefits of the sacrifices they say they've made.

The present is stronger than all.

It's the present of cinema, bull fighting, and tennis: three things I loved. It's an absolute that passes and re-passes, and which no one is able to possess. It was crazy to want an entire society to treat itself to a "bull's horn" for more than a month. What's ugly in football are the fans who come and scream for ninety minutes; what's beautiful in a bullfight is that it's enough for four passes to re-establish a current. The crowd is bored, chatting, and they seem far away. One good pass and a light silence is established. A second and you sense a slight inclination to accompany the stirrings of the final passes, the *faena*. A third and it's the first "olé," that which says it wants more. A fourth, and the whole audience finds itself in the spectacle, with this other "olé" that says you're satisfied ("*ich habe genug*").

I wonder if the cinematically vain 1980s in tennis weren't like the true cinema with pleasing heroes like Borg, Connors, McEnroe, and Lendl, the only ones who could *distill* time and give lessons on spectatorship to an entire generation. I was always surprised at my friends' astonishment at my ability to write about tennis, like I was upset with them for not understanding that it was the *same thing* as cinema, or at least an older cinema, that of *mise-en-scène* and topography. It wouldn't take much effort for me to find passing-shots in Fritz Lang and inserts with Miroslav Mecir.

Coming back to 1968, as I now see it, probably a little too clearly, after May and June I had more and more "experiences" of dispossession. First, travel: my first trip to India, that is to say, to the third world. Then, illness: my first bout with tuberculosis. The cinema had disappeared because I was experiencing *my* cinema on my own body as something not possessed. In fact cinema hadn't disappeared, it was I who, in some way, was in a film, for a few years playing the role of the incognito star on stages where there was no one to see me. My blockbusters, announced by postcard, were rather modest: I was the main actor in *I Arrive in Yemen*, and I was perfectly natural in *I Return to my Hotel in Taroudant.*

This period when you were traveling opens a parentheses in your relationship with Cahiers du cinéma. *It seems that just after, at the beginning of the 1970s, it was rather brutally put to you: come back to the journal, but only on the condition that you inherit it.*

Yes, and it seems like I awaited this inheritance for a very long time, without worrying too much. I must have confused those who made up *Cahiers*, who must not have understood anything that was for me already opaque. In fact I was very alone; having had only a tribe of women for an imposed family, I probably opted for a gang of men as my elected family. I explained why I recognized it immediately, but I should also say why it had such a hard time recognizing me, why I had to become the cleaning lady of *Cahiers* at the end of 1973 in order to warrant little by little, saying "we" before quitting to be able to say "I," and then today "me, myself." In this little book which tries to avoid—finally—dressing itself up in a "we" that is impossible to locate, I chose to avoid going into detail about "my relationships" with each of those who composed it—to do so would require psychoanalysis. What interests me here is that which renders a little more clearly in my eyes what I will call the "solution of cinema."

This family only existed in my head, which doesn't mean—after all—that my desire would end up making it real afterwards. It's a family without a father, just as it has to be in cinephilia, filial love towards an absent, dead, or weak father, exactly like Bazin. It's the dream of a family of equals and egos, the dream of "sublime brothers," which leads down the road of big mistakes and equally big wounds.

Coming back to my idea concerning French cinema, having the impression that it almost always misses its relation to the real, which will never function as the sentinel overseeing its own history, the history of France. For example, May '68 is an eruption that doesn't really concern it, except in it's militant, underground form, which finally produced Phillipe Garrel, who is the only filmmaker issued positively from '68. This French cinema has an odd tenor as if its originality was also its limit.

It's an alarming specter that I always understood, which is true and which nevertheless irritates me. It's true that Resnais appeared to me as someone who was pretty much of his time. But simultaneously we act as if there was a French case, the monstrous case of a country that always botched history. We say that France never filmed the Algerian War, and I say: have you ever seen a country filming its colonial war?

Did England film Gandhi when he was alive? The Americans, when they occupied Haiti and the Philippines, did they make films about these countries? No. The largest part of this human history, in the twentieth century of wars, wasn't filmed. And when we look for "good" examples, there are only two—certainly extraordinary—the American and the Italian. The former because cinema makes up part of their cultural genome, the latter because they had the capacity to *remake* a country, a face, between 1945 and 1960. All the same it's not much. And when we think of the immensity of the unshown and of the unseen in Russia, for example, we think that with this role the cinema did what it could and now that's behind us. Things can come back, but they have to come a first time. There's no foundational dimension of cinema in a nation-state as old as France. There is, on the other hand, the consciousness of having co-invented the cinema and having always been the recording room, the tribunal. We inherited that, and that's something. What's disgusting in the case of French cinema is how everyone drapes themselves in this negative exaggeration that leads them to believe that France alone would be able to tell the story of its own role in the century—which is, by the way, not so great. We no longer have the means since Abel Gance and the cinema of the trenches. There is a feeling of happiness, of breathing, of the simple fact of "being happy and seeing clearly" that I never found—except sporadically with Godard, Becker, or Demy—in French cinema. I never looked for it there. Inversely, I think that the children of the American circus, Buster Keaton or Fred Astaire, danced the possibility of being human on earth and in the end that touches me most of all.

Part III

CHAPTER 3

Cinema and History

Let's continue with the question of history. We're witnessing a return of history with which cinema is intimately mixed, and we'll soon be celebrating it's one hundredth anniversary. How do you account for the fact that in France cinema has had a hard time taking responsibility for its own history?

You can only respond trivially: the French state, like the English state, is a thousand years old, and the two have a point in common: a total lack of historical concern or anxiety. Why is it that Spain, which wasn't always Francoist, didn't make a considerable contribution to the history of cinema? Obviously, in these countries there's something along the lines of a foundation which doesn't present itself, a mythological project which isn't entirely open. And France, by bringing back first-hand the precious artifact but not the museum—unlike Italy and America, which built the museum—was thus the ethnographer of its own history and also the founder of cinema. It therefore has something to say on this point that it disputes with America. It's clear for the Americans that it was Edison and not the Lumière brothers who invented cinema. I'm afraid that with the centenary and the question of origins, France will be at the front-line of a battle where it will have to make its claim worthy of being the cradle of cinema, just as it was the cradle of photography. In some ways it's about its right to preemption regarding the history of cinema and photography. Except it has to reckon with the hypothesis according to which the end of the First World War must have signaled the end of a number of things in France. For instance, if a filmmaker as big as Abel Gance is today totally impractical for us, so unknown and so unwatched, it's perhaps because he belongs to an utterly completed nineteenth-century France. Even liberated, French cinema is more concerned with individuals. Which is precisely why we both love and hate it; it introduces us to a world-to-come which might no longer need the cinema: the world of individuals. That obviously doesn't constitute popular entertainment; it gets boring pretty quickly. So perhaps France represents an impasse, but the other countries aren't going to get around this impasse. It may seem like I take this question lightly, but it's done quite a number on me as it's the absence of Vichy, the absence of images of collaboration, which, over the course of many years, revealed itself to me as unacceptable. Today from a mystic and intransigent point of view, I would say that if cinema is the art of the present (in the widest sense, not only that of reporting, but also the present of calling in to memory, of evocation: for example the Straubs' films), then when it doesn't take place, it doesn't take place. This allows us to understand one thing: cinema exists only to bring back what has already been seen once: well seen, poorly seen, unseen. Ten years later *Nuit et brouillard* returns what wasn't seen, bearing in mind that the images of the camps filmed by George Stevens, or those assembled by Hitchcock, have been stashed away by the Americans and the English. In this capacity as an art of the present, or an art of vigilance, cinema was already suffering from severe schizophrenia, since the same people who ordered the images, the British and the Americans, were the same ones to put them aside due to the cold war. Even though they're just archival films, the only ones made at the time of the discovery, they have an enormous effect on us when we now watch them for the first time. The film that marked me, *Nuit et brouillard*, was made almost fifteen years after the discovery of the camps. The film inscribes itself in this delay as a work of art—Jean Cayrol's script, and Hanns Eisler's music—a work of extraordinary precision and taste. But it's possible that this rhetoric resembles the rhetoric of the tracking shot in *Kapo*. Accordingly many important things concerning the fate of the people, nations and masses, were strictly not seen, in order to be able to return. I'm afraid that this isn't definitive. I remember meeting Chris Marker in Hong Kong and he was excited to learn that the red guards had filmed. We always wondered what they could have filmed; today it remains an anecdotal question: it's not important. There was a time when things took time to exist, across slow, difficult, and painful processes: it took time to build, and this time had value. Today the benefits have to be seen immediately. Maybe cinema had the capacity to make synchronic or histological cuts, seizing the work of time—not just death at work, but men at work. For example, over the course of fifteen years Italian cinema showed us the architectural reconstruction of a country, passing from the ruins to the first slabs of concrete, and then to the ugliness of contemporary post-modernism: it was seen through a stroboscopic, jerky movement. For us, Tati was the only one who every five years gave us a kind of physical report about the landscapes we were living in, and they were always more surprising than the old image we still held. Ultimately, I don't think cinema ever had another genius than him or had more dignity than that.

We're returning to cinema strictly conceived of as an art of recording.

We can only record the present, a present that is confusing in so far as it is taken as an idea, myth, or dream of a process that we don't have to see or verify everyday. Doesn't the malaise of information in the media come from the fact that what is concurrent today is no longer cinema proper, but rather the observer and ceaseless surfer of these images? I repeat: the idea of the work of time, of the work of humanity, is incomprehensible today. As if what was left *on lease* in cinema, the power to prolong or accelerate things, and to make cuts, was progressively removed from it so that ultimately it became just like everything else in society. The problem is that it doesn't know exactly what to do with what's now coming back. Today it's up to tele-viewers to intelligently flip through the images of Yugoslavia. And if Emir Kusturica, a very good filmmaker, courageously makes a historical fiction film, *Vukovar Open City*, I doubt that the film will go anywhere else but Cannes. This circle, that of *Rome, Open City*, is, I believe, closed for the whole world, even if the French are the ones who are most conscious of it, and they remain *only* conscious. This explains why, at decisive moments, the French identity acts theatrically: it's not cinema that decides. There's a Robert Capa photograph that has always blown me away, the one of the shorn woman at Chartres during the Liberation. For me it's one of the most beautiful photographs ever taken. Precisely at this moment Capa is a more amazing filmmaker than he is a photographer. What does he show? A city, the theater of an entire city, with an effect of flattening the space: in the first shot everyone is pointing at this woman, the majority have their backs turned to her, except for a few who are near her. It's like a theater seen in reverse by an American; you get the impression that the whole city of Chartres is outside, there's a big space where everyone is looking at this woman who will very soon be *off*. For me it's theater. Do you remember that unforgettable shot in Godard's *Ici et Ailleurs*, with the little Palestinian girl on the ruins reciting a poem by Mahmoud Darwich; and Godard's voice-over saying, "This little girl continues '89."[1] That brings back an imaginary in which I grew up, which I loved as a child trembling with fear: the Revolution as it was taught to us by the secular. This is how France plays out its identity, because it hasn't found a better ritual than the theater; than this way of always repeating something, which refers to what it means for us to live together, to remember and to purge together. Contrary to cinema, where there is no catharsis, theater brings about the return of gestures, figures, and attitudes, the kinds of lines we all would have liked to say: "We are here by the will of the people ..."

Ultimately the New Wave didn't create new characters, attitudes, or a new repertoire of gestures. It was perhaps content to singularize and redistribute roles, by integrating a certain American mythology, that of B movies or "Film Noir." Today even with the best French film, something doesn't and can't take: you never get the feeling that a story happens to just anybody. In your opinion, does everything come from theater?

We ask ourselves about the things that preoccupy us today: a return of history, in Malet and Isaac's[2] sense of the term. The New Wave (in France in particular, but also throughout the New Waves of the world) was stuck with doing something completely different: a man and a woman, the war of the sexes, and the eventual resolution of this war. Between 1960 and 1980 all artistic and creative energy is invested there. The cinema of ideals, the masculine cinema (only men have ideals), had to be exchanged for a cinema that would allow women to appear. Antonioni, Bergman, and of course Godard did nothing other than this. Pialat spent a lot of energy doing it, Rivette in his own way, and Rohmer, Ferreri, Cassavetes, etc. It was the problem of couples, above all heterosexual couples; then after '68 came the idea of incompatible, disparate, Deleuzian couples (*Alice in the Cities*). The idea of the couple is central—remember how we wanted to do an issue of *Cahiers* on domestic quarrels? This remains the central idea, in terms of content, even if it's far from us, because we're in a strange sort of post-feminist era where things reconstruct themselves in a different way. The big shocks for the filmmakers of the New Wave were the appearance of Brigitte Bardot, the photograph of Harriet Andersson, or Monica Vitti (we were a long way from Michèle Morgan), images of women who insisted that they couldn't be filmed as before. This occupied cinema for fifteen or twenty years; it was moving the language, even the films from Lelouch's *girly* side (*Un Homme et une femme*.) All of which is to say that our historic concern today is not pertinent, nor was it the motive force of that cinema, and unless we rewrite history we can't reproach it for that.

I wanted to point out a difference between French and American, or even Italian, cinema: the character, whether it's with Ford or Capra, exists as much as the star does, or at least it's not totally confused with the star. In French cinema, the character is almost necessarily an archetype, even Belomondo in Breathless.

Right, it can never be a place-holder for the civic conscience. You find those characters in America and in Italy, which are two countries that had to be established or reestablished.

It seems to me that at one time Jean Gabin was able to incarnate a kind of heroic and popular figure, whether in the films of Jean Renoir or Marcel Carné. But that remains an exception. Today the starification of Gérard Depardieu isn't the same: it is an absolute element of our cinema that never allows us to recognize the real singularity of the character or citizen. The fisherman in Stromboli *is really a fisherman. In France the documentary, or the documentary-like, has always been ridiculed.*

I wouldn't say ridiculed but hypostasized. There *is* documentary in *Toni* like there is documentary in the best French films: for example in the work of Bresson or Gremillion. But it's *of* documentary, like we say of ore—in its pure state. In *Gueule d'amour*, which I adore, the first twenty shots are very disparate; we see to what extent Gremillion is a nut, what comes out of him is a kind of madness. So in these twenty shots there are three or four that could be found in Carné, and two others in Rouquier. It's an element specific to French cinema to be able to propose only rarefied and pure states of things, through documentary or fiction, and not to know how to make pasta, this sort of *grande bouffe* that only Italy for some time and America—because it's all European—for an even longer time knew how to make. Unfortunately the matter is settled quickly. Why Americans? Let's take two of the most important films of my life, I saw them both in 1959, and I continue to adore them: Preminger's *Anatomy of a Murder* and Hitchcock's *North by Northwest*. Their common point is the character of the big fool; one is very obvious in the case of Cary Grant, the other more subtle in the case of Jimmy Stewart. Stewart's character doesn't do anything, he just goes fishing, and then over the course of two hours and forty minutes, he finds his old career as a lawyer. He relearns how to be sly, except that in front of Lee Remick he's lost, he no longer knows what a woman is. Only America was capable of showing the faces of innocents—it's not the man in the street, it's not the ideological *qualunquisme*:[3] someone who isn't as clever as the script when the film begins, but who catches up *before* us, without any shame of being a citizen just like us. There's this inherent trait in the citizen: a citizen by status and not because it's a role, upon whose head a certain number of tiles fall. Before it evolved too much, American cinema created unforgettable and incomparable portraits, with big actors playing the confused and representing our interests as citizens: citizens in so far as it is someone whom we ask at a given moment to become conscious of a law, and if he's a good citizen, to choose a side and then act. In terms of fiction and narration, it's a character who is one step behind, and this tardiness is the length of the film and will give him enough time to catch up. This is a long way from French cinema, which is a cinema of the clever, where the essential thing is that the figure of the holy monster is one step ahead and that he maintains this lead.

CHAPTER 4

Cinephile in Transit

Let's go back to the travel years: there's a moment in your life where travel replaces cinema. Unless perhaps for you travel is also a form of recording images.

Provided that I don't take them [the pictures].

I mean images in the sense of "mental images." I don't picture you walking around with a camera.

Obviously the preparation of the bag is essential, it's the traveler's neurosis: leaving with the least amount of stuff possible. It's the fantasy of the traveler without luggage, totally self-sufficient in his dispossession. He who, in my case in particular, knows how to do absolutely nothing. Traveling means walking, or looking at a map, or going from a café to the train station, or looking for a hotel, sometimes visiting two or three things, losing myself in the city, all regardless of how much money I have. Towards the end I took taxis; in the beginning I walked. Thus the traveler without luggage, the citizen of the world: we return to this word "citizen." The citizen of the world is at home everywhere as soon as he is no longer at home. Most people begin to feel afraid or uneasy as soon as they leave home. For me it's the opposite: I could be uneasy or anxious where I belonged, that is to say, in Paris, but auratically blessed or struck by a kind of divine protection as soon as I was somewhere else; persuaded that nothing could happen to me as long as I was clandestine, being nothing and having nothing. That's how I found myself at the end of the world, in impossible or even dangerous corners: it wasn't out of bravery but simply because there was a map and a street that led me there. I couldn't accept the idea that there were forbidden countries. I'm sad now that I can't go to the countries that have just opened themselves, like Ulan Bator, who knows. I know very well what I would do in Ulan Bator: nothing. I would send a postcard, and I would have loved it. In traveling, there is the idea of being reduced to one's own body. I had this fantasy of leaving without luggage and buying everything I needed at the airport. Not having your home with you and saying to yourself, "The world is my country, and the airports its supermarkets." Recently my friend Gérard Dupuy[1] and I were asking ourselves what we would do if we were rich, and all we could come up with was this fantasy of having ten well-chosen studios all across the world, from Mayfair in London, Central Park in New York, Marrakech, Cairo, Tokyo, Barcelona, Berlin, the cities where we would love to live, and going anonymously from one to the next. The essential thing being that we leave no trace, no images: being clandestine in this world.

The word "clandestine" allows us to come back to cinema: there is evidently clandestinity in cinephilia itself, the cinephilia that you lay claim to.

Cinema allowed for this kind of clandestinity, as opposed to theater, which insists on appearing before my neighbors and peers, who are also citizens. Without a doubt theater can't disappear, even if it isn't in such great shape. I'm being unfair because I did pursue the TNP (Théâtre national populaire)[2] programming for a year or two, and even that marked me quite a bit. Vilar[3] was unforgettable, but the nightmare for me, at 10 or 11 years old, was the Comedie-Française: I was terrorized. Oddly enough the circus didn't impress me (I didn't go to the circus and it wasn't until much later that I was blown away seeing Fellini's *The Clowns*). But I'll never forget the terror of that sound of the floor-boards, the footsteps of the actors: boom, boom … And then a more erotic feeling, almost already misogynist, when the serving girls, with their breasts showing, entered howling so that the gallery could hear them. It has to be said that those rhetorical and clumsy introductions to such and such a work by Molière never made me laugh at all—one should have the courage to say that the comic works of Molière aren't really that funny any more. This terror, this whole social ritual, the French language with its have-you-seen-me side, the obligation to remain upright like one's neighbor, the impossibility of being clandestine: all that horrified me. Gradually I made up with theater, always loving filmed theater, which has its advantages without its disadvantages, or let's say without its essence. Guitry never made me uncomfortable, and his recording of something which says "no" to recording is what is most beautiful in his films, and much more troubling than Pagnol's. I was able to reclaim the theater via cinema; I invented a protective screen that prevents theater from disturbing me (or impassioning me, as with Oliveira), because it is a reservoir of shared aesthetic hypotheses between theater and cinema, without which cinema would die. For about ten years I've understood that, reduced to its recording-terror side, cinema lived what it had to live, that it didn't have a follow-up, that it logically lost its audience, and that it had to continue in order for its other side to become strong, the side which is incarnated by Bergman or Fassbinder. It's also the reason why I like Gus Van Sant's films (*My Own Private Idaho*), that this kid comes from the theater and in only ten shots succeeds at what Zeffirelli had tried to create his entire life. Today I give practically no credence to the mystical recording. I certainly see that we will not rip the phenomena of ritual out of the theater, the collective identity, the lived and relived history; that's its domain, it will either do it well or it won't, but I see less and less how that concerns cinema. Cinema's capacity to witness, to-be-there-in-the-present, having almost disappeared for a while, finds itself with the obligation to invent imaginary worlds, to explore the mental. For me Kubrick is the great filmmaker of the mental. The problem is that this question of the present has to be reconsidered.

Let's come back to travel: do you find the experience of traveling or walking in certain filmmakers more than others, for example from those who are little marginalized, or who work alone?

I don't have any problem with Robert Kramer: seeing *Route One* I recognize the way one sees when walking. For me walking is very close to speech. I began walking systematically rather late in life, before I walked obsessively, like Poe's "The Man of the Crowd," incapable of stopping myself. Then I understood that it was possible to follow itineraries. It became the greatest possible pleasure for me, unfortunately too late, where I'm able to grasp my absolute reality, whereas before it was a sort of compulsion much stronger than I was. I see this experience of walking very clearly in *The Night of the Hunter*, it's an experience of time, it's a miniaturized experience—almost infantile or derisory—of the great scripts of revelation. It so happens that I have a very good topographical memory, much more so than a genuine sense of orientation; that's why I'm able to retain the memory of where my body has been. My greatest trip on foot was in Tuscany five years ago, one of the most beautiful corners of the world, and one of the most practical for walking. Certain trips were successful and others failed, but sometimes it rains and then suddenly the sun comes up, you have the map and then ... I'm going to tell you an anecdote, which I wanted to turn into a chapter for the book, where in complete consciousness I understood what for me walking, travel, and cinema had in common. Sometimes I preferred walking, that is to say, talking with my legs, over speaking, which is to say, walking with my mouth—but basically it's the same thing.

CHAPTER 5

A Night in Ronda

One night I'm in Spain on a train that stops in Ronda. At Málaga I bought a pair of shoes, and at Bodilla I dutifully changed trains. I was moving quickly towards Andalucia dulled by the month of February. *Nothing in the hands, nothing in the pockets*, according to the adage, and I should add: *nothing in the head and everything in the legs*, because the legs want to walk. The five letters of the word Ronda, the bullfighting capital, turn in my head like ossicles which, just like dice, don't abolish chance. It's my provisional end of the world. I wait to see the passage from the word to the thing, knowing—I've been traveling for a while—that all pleasure resides in this present that is *wedged* between a past and a future equally without weight. As a spectator, I "saw nothing at Hiroshima"; as a traveler on firm ground, I would obviously see "nothing at Ronda."

In my compartment there are a few taciturn soldiers with shaved heads. In front of me a pretty kid and his girlfriend. They hardly notice me, to the point that I can stare at them as if there was no one in my place. Every traveler, and every cinephile as well, knows moments where, like a purloined letter, he is in the middle of a picture, both nothing and superimposed, a willing hostage to the movement which ignores him. Seeing a film isn't traveling, it's taking the first train that arrives, getting off at the station where the name is pleasing, deciding everything backwards: that it was *this* station, *this* train, and *this* night, sullen and thick, finally fallen when you arrive at the destination. Who will recount the pleasure of having forgotten the name of this? Ah yes, Ronda.

That night the doubling was such that I saw myself. Instead of being the last one off the train with the confused look of someone from somewhere else, instead of consulting a map or asking for information, I followed the soldiers who confidently returned home. Having my modest gray sack by its strap in order to move faster, I rushed out of the station without looking at anything or anyone as if I was also annoyed by this local train's late arrival in Ronda. It was a choice between left or right, and to hesitate was to lose the tempo, was to put down the bag and no longer resolutely move away from the center of town. But I did nothing, following the meager flux of travelers and remarking in the transition that they were sinking into silence in the deserted streets and bits of poorly lit asphalt. I understood that I was *nowhere*, a nowhere that happened to be Ronda, but which could have been just as easily Villepinte in France, or Culemborg in Holland. So I went 2,000 kilometers to get the sense of being "home," in a sort of universal suburb. Like in Fellini's films, I walked for a while and it seemed like I was getting close to my destination, when I understood that I had "returned." Returned to a world which, catapulted to the center of Ronda, is quickly about to sober up amidst a costumed crowd, because it was carnival. I spent the night in a poorly heated little room at the "Reina Victoria" hotel, and it wasn't until morning that I discovered the austere splendor of this far-away Andalusia that I hadn't seen the day before. When I was finally "home," and settled, with the assistance of postcards, this mix of the map and the territory promised by the two syllables of the word "Ronda," I was able to begin casting about the stupefied gaze of the average tourist and I quickly discovered that I had nothing to do in this very pretty city of Ronda. Then Sanlucar de Barrameda, the other bullfighting capital, even more secret—with its "El Bigote" bar at the seashore—became the end of the world.

Did it occur to you that the real had given you a gift, and that you just had to accept it?

Yes, with the idea that what I was going to take wouldn't be missed by anyone. I'm grateful for people existing and for the world being there. At the same time, I really have the feeling that it's the world which exists and not me, that I try very hard to exist in this world. But I have concerns about the existence of this world; I see it clearly, this poorly lit little train station in Ronda, while the regular tourist doesn't want to have anything to do with it because it doesn't make up part of his experience. Cinema taught me one thing: that the most beautiful scenes or the most beautiful shots begin with a little scene of nothing at all, like this one, equally as important as the big scenes. Since I don't really like bravura, I always need passage from one to the other. Via my body and this experience of walking I'm happy to be the *passeur*: to go from one disappointing shot to another which will remain. Fellini is great in so far as he never films bravura without showing the before and after shot; this is what I learned to like about him—he thinks his films out according to the logic of the walker.

For example, when he films a party, or a carnival scene, there's always a before and after image, with a kind of desolation that follows euphoria.

The walker is the one who accepts that the show has always already begun. His slowness insists upon it, like the fact that everything he will discover happens according to its own rhythm: the ant perceived in the grass where you were sitting, tired, was already there in front of you, but you simply couldn't see it. I worked most of my life to get rid of this sense of almost paranoid guilt, which made me think I should have seen it. I can laugh at it today, because now I know how to enjoy my part a little better. But for a long time the idea of spending each day in the same place without seeing what was obvious, some unbelievable luminous sign, or some other element of the décor, seemed to me to be a disavowal of myself. I needed someone to show me; that's why I couldn't have a simple relationship to the image. I'm not at all a visionary; I'm more the type of person who has to have things shown to him. Or who, in order to see, needs to invent complicated scenarios for himself, which at some point pass through his body, by walking for example. Back to the question of the frame: I have a lot of trouble seeing what isn't framed. I fully realize that a frame doesn't just make itself, it expresses the will or desire of he who wants to show: "You will look at this!" Thus my problem with the theater, which doesn't depend on a frame, and which for me becomes synonymous with audio-visual fatigue. It's a problem of perceptual slowness, but as soon as the frame exists I'm quick.

Last question about traveling: are you ever tempted to stay, to sort of become one with the landscape?

Never. I always had the fantasy of returning, and in many cities, I thought: this is great, I'm going to come back and really get to know this city, finally get to know it in all its detail. Morocco is the only country that I deliberately returned to, assured of a kind of physical welcoming. Otherwise I always assumed that what I didn't already know was better. The things that I didn't know are the words that have their own truth: Jakarta is an immense horrible city made of concrete, uninhabitable and extremely poor, but I knew the word "Jakarta" since I was 6 years old. My problem is choosing between the word and the thing. Sometimes after the experience of the thing I don't maintain a strong memory of it: it's questionable, debatable. As if the *jouissance* and the experience of things were always put off until tomorrow. What is important is the meeting: was my arrival in ______ a success? I remember arriving in Havana at three in the morning, a phantasmatic crossing of the city in the middle of the night, people already lined up for the bus, and my staying in a big hotel. As if it wasn't even a question of going to sleep, I watched daybreak, to see what this city I had just crossed looked like. It's an idea of engagement, the promise of a world with which I am eternally engaged, which happens though words, cities, maybe boys, postcards, and which I scribbled down in notebooks. It's a terribly minimal and perverse conception of travel, which doesn't correspond at all to the image of the great traveler that my friends have of me. The more time that passes, the more the feeling of needing to go to the end of the world diminishes: there is no country that I dreamed of as a child that I didn't go to. It would have been a disaster if I hadn't gone to China, to Japan, or to Brazil. Most recently I've wanted to cross France on foot, since it's the country I know the least. The French landscape resembles French cinema: it's very beautiful but you need to find the right method: either by train, or by car, because the country is too small by TGV. Italy, England, France, Belgium, and Germany: that's what I would have done. For me Europe implied traveling by foot; it was my plan, to feel slow and small in relation to what's bigger than me. I wouldn't go to Tirana, or Ljubljana, the capital of Slovenia, and that's fine. One day I'd really like to feel small again, exploring the Ardèche: I know it's beautiful.

Is there a link for you between the themes of traveling and flirting?

There are these encounters that are amusing and touching, and because they're furtive and futureless they take on the true dimension of a mournful camaraderie. While sexually it was pitiful, I have a very vivid memory of it—that has nothing to do with the profitability of pleasure. It's the sad consolation of the lone and clandestine flirter, but it's sometimes very engrossing. I once thought that a boy's sex helped me frame my gaze, that it was a point of departure for seeing something else, what allowed me to eroticize the world, and to give it a north and a south. As soon as you see a good-looking kid in the corner, there is immediately a center and a perimeter, thus a shot, and that's an image: a boy's presence creates an image. It's what I'm able to say about everything that is of the order of erotic investment, or what we were saying about a character. Never in my life did I identify with Cary Grant, but the films in which I liked Cary Grant are those in which his presence created an image: all the rest was organized around him. It's therefore a principle of a general erotic orientation, where eroticism is a means and not an end.

Do the boys help you see a country better? Are they guides in some way?

In the third world they're guides by nature. There are two periods of my travels: between 1968 and let's say my arrival at *Libération* was a time of traveling poor, and then after. Before, I had taken a number of big trips, almost completely broke, one to India and another to Africa which lasted almost a year, then three or four months in Darkest Africa. At *Cahiers* I was lucky enough that no argued with me about the plane tickets that were always showing up. One day I found myself in Jakarta, and then finally in Surabaya, invited by someone from the embassy who thought I was André Bazin. Later I visited the third world through the other door, that of palaces. At *Libération* I traveled a lot, but a little wealthier. When traveling poor it was easy to meet boys on the street, whether in the Arab world, Dark Africa, or Asia.

And since they had to sell themselves as half-prostitutes, they served as guides, generally bad, but I didn't care, since I'm not the slightest bit interested in taking in monuments. For example, Arab boys are in general pretty bad lovers, but they are very touching because they have the same colonial culture as we do, and their relationship to knowledge is real. With my big brother or teacher side, I have some wonderful memories of the young men in Medina to whom I gave English lessons. We would read Coleridge together in bed. It's Gide-like in the sense that sexually it's a little overwhelming. Basically there is one great rule: birds of a feather flock together. And it often happened that I would come across a group of young boys, like there often are in these countries, a gang of young boys making a lot of noise, and in the middle of them there is always one who is silent. That's the one who always comes to me; I would always end up recognizing him. There is this sort of universality of he who will never be a part of the pack. It's very narcissistic to find yourself disguised in a young third world boy, but it's also true. I never really had any big mishaps (in general I'm not particularly risky, but sometimes I was), maybe because of a certain assurance of being superimposed on the landscape, because of a certain doubt of really existing, matched with the certainty that the world for its part did exist. In the experience of the stroller-flirter-stroller this sense of barely existing is so strong that it protects him; a feeling that is often light, and which writers have written about better—for example Robert Walser or Rimbaud. Cinema is composed only of those who operate according to a truth of walking. The image of little boy who wants to kill Robert Mitchum and watches him walk by on horseback from the grange where he's sleeping remains fundamental for me. Because there is the truth of walking, of progression: the children who have come by boat, the other on horseback, they move by and large to the same rhythm.

CHAPTER 6

Cinema Would be the Promise of the World

I'd like to come back to culture and the way you have of thinking cinema, or cinephilia, within a vast ensemble of what would be culture. If I understand it right, cinema became the promise of a world, it was synonymous with an opening on to the world, via the voyages that consist of going to verify elsewhere that others live this same experience of the cinema, but through other languages. Could you tell me about this cultural passage?

For many of my generation, culture was the great idea, the great opportunity or invention, the great secular belief. I remember flipping through Élie Faure's *Histoire de l'art* and André Malraux's books at the public library, which were the promise of a knowledge because they traced a line that went from Lascaux to Goya and passed through African art. That meant that everything was possible, that we were saved. Like everyone at that time I grew up in the post-war climate, lulled by the ideology of "Popular Education," which was, I realize today, a kind of gospel or solace. It gave us permission to no longer be religious while maintaining a relationship to the sacred, cultivating oneself, learning and being curious. This vision *à la* Malraux and Faure, to which Godard is the heir, gave permission to get out of the West, not to be limited by it, to have a global and generous conception of culture, and to allow for the welcoming of all that humankind had produced as objects that could be considered as art. They had to somehow be phased in, and this work justified a lifetime. That's what I had to tell myself unconsciously. The other idea of culture is more biographical: I come from a family where during my childhood there couldn't have been more than twenty books in the house. My mother read very little, and yet she had a great respect for culture. The family milieu was less closed or anti-cultural than invertebrate: composed only of women who knew nothing and had difficult lives. There was nothing. I was in charge of the cultural spirit for the family. I remember the day that I bought the Brandenburg Concertos, one of the great shocks you can have at around 12 or 13 years old, and no one in the house had ever heard them: it was the absolute, marvelous. It was the same thing with cinema. I would go arm in arm with my mother and grandmother to see Mizoguchi's films at the defunct Studio Bertrand. I had total confidence in *Cahiers*, which wrote that these films were great, and I can see us arriving late on a Sunday, our day to go out, getting totally lost transferring in the subway, and the credits for *Tales of Ugetsu* already scrolling on the screen. I was seized by a holy terror. What I experienced there was by no means banal and it explains the obligation that I was always to be my own teacher: no one played this role in my life, and I was never going to let anyone.

The idea that you would go far never occurred to your mother or grandmother?

As far as I can tell it was never talked about. They were proud of me just for being and sure that I was going to get an education. An education was the demarcating line: I thus participated in a desirable world, a world that the people desired.

But no one talked about the idea of a career?

I don't think my mother really had plans for me, I think I even remember her saying that manual trades were great and that one day I could be a carpenter. I recently told her this and it annoyed her: "That's not true! I wanted you to be a lawyer!" I remember a teacher in a gray shirt, the sublime Mr. Doumick, who called her to the school to tell her that her kid should definitely go to high school. At that time my mother was just satisfied that I existed, my family was so happy just to finally have a nice little boy who resembled his father, and who represented something a little marvelous, that they truly forgot to have the shadow of an aspiration for me. Which undoubtedly explains why I spent my life without plans or ambition. I was completely carefree since my birth alone fulfilled my essential function; people were oddly content just to see me arrive here on earth. I was thus a very poor and very spoiled child. Later on I became conscious of what made things difficult for me, since I always had to invent the question in order to come up with the answer. I must have created the concept of culture at home. And it couldn't be bourgeois culture, but that of the whole world, which was written about, for example, in George Sadoul's *History of Cinema*, the only book that made me dream of cinema, in spite of its foolishness and typos. Culture wasn't what gave me society—that might be the difference between you and me—but rather what gave me the world. And then there was cinema. It wasn't a question of daring to say coldly that thanks to culture I was going to write in the margins of this world, on the side that I was born on. Bourgeois society was always the enemy, or at least I always distrusted it—*they're not friends*, as they say in Renoir. Even before the love of cinema there was already the idea that there would be no culture without a promise that would concern the entire civilization, which would go in all directions and all times, of which I would be able to be my own teacher: he who discovers the questions at the same time as the answers. When I began to read *Arts*, André Parinaud's weekly, with a passion, I started to make little synoptic tables with columns, like in the Pléiade:[1] painting, literature, music, and cinema. With the information surveyed in *Arts* I acted as if it was the entire Byzantine Empire, and I was in charge of cataloging it. Developing oneself to this point "outside of the symbolic" is incredible and I am almost astonished that I was just a nice little pervert and not a total criminal. It was logical that I looked for what created rules, and what created faith, having benefited so much from an imaginary Oedipal incest. Indeed doubly incestuous, since my grandmother had an existential authority over my mother. Everything was pieced together and negotiated amongst women; it was a tribe that was very conscious of not being like the neighbors (the concept of neighbors was the *absolute* elsewhere).

I remember you began to earn a living rather late, when we were working together at Cahiers *at the beginning of the 1970s. How did you get along before that?*

I had grants and I lived with my mother, a little like I was living at a hotel. For a long time she gave me pocket money, very little, and then she stopped. I got my clothes from the flea market; it was the age of velvet jackets—I loved that, there was never anything better. I always absolutely believed that money problems wouldn't ruin my life, because I had pleasures and desires that I was able to give myself. The whole cinemathèque period was one outside of economy: subways, cheap tickets, and cafés. Returning home at 4 in the morning, I always found some can of stew that my mother had left for me. I lived absolutely outside of economy. Without that I would have never accepted that first pitiful salary *Cahiers* offered me.

I remember, it was miraculous.

(*Laughter*) Yeah. Before going to *Libération*, I never knew what a crisp bill was. I always traveled at my own expense, even when I was at *Cahiers*. I found it so amazing that I never abused it; it was something of a miracle: the goodness of the other. I often return to this question of culture, because it could seriously be asked again today, this sort of cultural ideal that lost its absolute innocence. It's something I share with Jean-Claude Biette,[2] for example, having been fished out, like a lot of children of the general public, without asking them how they're going to get along in the jungle of society. That doesn't stop me from seeing how much it's degraded, recomposed, or that the Bovaryism of this question is likely to be asked poorly. If culture is a promise, it's that of having the experience of great works, not just an apprenticeship of knowledge. Just like postcards or a map, the promise always exceeds what you will actually experience. I thus always had the feeling of a possible sham in looking at some nice book full of reproductions of paintings, only to strut about in a milieu that I ended up frequenting, where it's not a question of admitting that one has simply forgotten to look at the originals. Ultimately I lived with the idea that this promise was made up of proper names, proper names being the promise of experience, regardless of whether or not the experience had been had—and this ended up by circulating in a world that asked not to see. It's a problem of belief: in a time when people were more religious, they weren't questioned about reality, or giving proof. Absolute hypocrisy was possible. Since Flaubert, culture has allowed for similar things, impostures. It's one of the reasons why I was so stuck on the Straubs' films, not so much because of the terror, but rather out of admiration for someone who said: we will move forward step by step, by taking the people there where they are.

In culture one goes by foot.

Yes, we go by foot: the sandals of Jean-Marie Straub. There would be a listening state there, which we can describe, even if it isn't brilliant. There would be a state of listening, a state of the eye, a state of the human body, and a state of texts. All of that would be described without imposture, and cinema would be able to take a step forward. When I think about Straub that's pretty much what I hold on to.

As if you were privileging a form of classical materialism?

Yes, or sensualism. With Straub and Huillet, the sensualism would have to be kept and the communism left behind. My favorite film of theirs is the Pavese adaptation *From the Clouds to the Resistance*; it's the one I found most convincing about the gods of antiquity, a subject of which I am pretty ignorant. Then there is *Moise et Aaron*: one Jewish leg and one Greek, the Christians having created the synthesis. They are undoubtedly right to think that culture had something to do with the two, and it is our fate to bear the weight of this vacillation. If the Straubs' films played the role of the superego for us, it was for pedagogical reasons: they are the wonderful professors that we would have liked to have had or be, who, using audio-visual objects, make real human experience possible, an experience that needs to be created one step at a time and with great exigency. Twenty years ago Straub and Huillet denounced the pimps of culture, like what you're doing today speaking to me about television and its generalized rite of passage; it's the same idea, which not only remains true but has gotten even worse. Cultural workers and the broadcasting systems have gone over to the side of a rite of passage that no longer knows itself.

In terms of my "glorious" cultural origins—my self-appointment between the Brandenburg Concertos and the Impressionists—I have to say that a page has turned. Why did I choose the cinema if I was more cut out to be a literature professor? In the cinema of the 1970s, did they not have this wonderful idea of a clandestine culture inside Culture with a capital C, where cinema had already entered? Once again I had to avoid society, or rather I had the desire to move across it, beginning with one of its great popular, but totally underestimated productions. It was this: choosing American westerns, the burlesque, or what was considered to make up popular culture, and then putting them in their proper place, which is to say, very high. It was to talk about *Beyond a Reasonable Doubt* while citing Heidegger. It was Rohmer using Kierkegaard to write about Hitchcock, who at the time was considered a hack. I found myself in that wager, what was at once the recognition of a popular being in the cinema and an unlimited becoming in the heights of culture. And I would never have been able to make this wager with opera or the theater.

What do you think of this idea, developed by others, that cinema offered all the other arts united into one, giving the best possible p.o.v.?

It was always a bit beyond me; I never really adhered to it theoretically speaking. I remember an article by Luc Moullet who said "the cinema cultivates us." We could say it today about television, although that wouldn't take us very far. For me it was rather to watch the films of Welles before reading Shakespeare, to see *The Tarnished Angels* before reading Faulkner: to make a culture out of what cinema itself could cross, adaptations, etc.

Cinema in so far as it made this great cultural promise possible and prosaic.

That's why I find this love of cinema in the twentieth century rather strange and beautiful. It's a true paradox: when I started becoming a cinephile, I was on the avant-garde's side in everything, I was for the most anti-bourgeois form, systematically, beyond all personal interest or pleasure. I never really frequented the world of music, but the names John Cage or Elliot Carter were burned into me without really being familiar with the music (I forgot to verify). So we were on the avant-garde's side in everything except cinema. And that hasn't changed, I don't really have the taste for experimental film, even if I think that there are interesting things happening there. I always loved those who were marginal, the directors working in their corner, and for me that hasn't changed. The American underground, which is a sector with no connection to Hollywood, has never really existed for me, and that's not something I'm proud of. But, for me, cinema wasn't about finding itself in arrogant isolation, cut off from everything, where there's no longer any nourishing of the imaginary. That finally explains this sort of hesitant waltz in the history of *Cahiers*, between Rohmer–Douchet on one side and Rivette–Labarthe on the other. The latter were historically correct: it was necessary to move towards the avant-garde. Except that the cinema prolonged something of the nineteenth century in the twentieth century for a very long time and in a rather unexpected manner. And it wouldn't have done so if entire generations hadn't been interested in enacting this prolongation. Some time was needed for the nineteenth-century narratives to exhaust themselves, whether it was the melodrama, vaudeville, or the circus. For us cabaret was definitively exhausted with *Playtime*, and maybe with Woody Allen for the United States; still it's all very recent. In this sense Schefer was right to say that cinema touches a very old part of us; moreover, the love of cinema today, when the two of us are speaking about it, appeared like a sort of defensive patriotism: we don't want a single thing to disappear. As if the memory of the nineteenth century and all of the twentieth century was there, and not somewhere else, and it was quite a job not to lose track of it, knowing what's going to unfold, what's there, but not yet able to pinpoint it.

According to this logic, cinephilia will possibly be the cultural form under which one will have attempted to prolong, for as long as possible, this state of cinema as a popular art form that doesn't yet consider itself an art. Will cinephilia become by nature defensive, and—we may as well say it—archaic?

It was cinema that allowed me to belong to my class, or perhaps more a status than a class: the poor. It was as simple as that: there were the poor and the rich; we were poor, which is to say, the little ones. My grandmother had a wonderful way of laughing at it. It's not at all a rueful memory, it's a particularly happy and ironic enough feeling, to be the little ones and to find some sort of pride in that: making your own way and not owing anything to anybody. Cinema allowed one to have a finger in every pie, to skirt society by stealing one of its popular products, without sharing it with society, keeping it all for ourselves. This explains why there is a cinephilic international: we're able to connect without any problems with the popular American productions, while none of us are American. It's ours the same way that jazz is ours, even if that doesn't hold: we're not black, but who cares? If someone steals Billie Holliday from me, someone steals the base upon which everything else is able to exist. And in front of this desire the enemy is always the same: the "Mr. Homais,"[3] those who don't believe, or who believe they know. It's quite simple, the human being produces works, and we will do what we have to with them, we make them serve us. This feeling was very strong with cinema, at a time when French cinema was discredited, not having produced even minor forms worthy of itself—frankly I don't think we need to keep fishing out Noël-Noël or Yves Deniaud.

Perhaps the great French cinema was somewhat aristocratic even in its essence: whether it's Renoir, Bresson, Ophuls, or Tati, these filmmakers are all pretty far from being petit-bourgeois.

In the case of French cinema I was always for the aristocrats, as if in terms of class, America and Italy were the one's who gave us the democratic ideals. We have always granted Italy a quality of popular or even vulgar emotion, but with an incredibly good will. The same holds for America. It was fine for me that it didn't exist in a French form, the cinema encouraging in me only the aristocratic part, that part composed of the filmmakers capable of refusal. The aristocracy was a way of forcefully saying no, as with Bresson in *Les Dames du bois de Boulogne*, or painfully like Gremillon, or this way of saying no while running away like Renoir. But I was never reconciled with the hum of regular French cinema, I really love this country but something never quite took hold. Perhaps it's simply because my father wasn't French.

CHAPTER 7

Cinema and Communism: In Defense of a Counter-society

When you speak of rich and poor, we are far from the Marxist rhetoric that speaks about social classes. Yet, when you were at Cahiers, *Marxism was an imposed figure. Ultimately the further we move away from that period of time the less I understand how you could have participated in the post-'68 political moment, with a language that isn't yours, and which was taken up by the journal. In thinking about this episode, which only lasted a few years, how do you reconstruct it today?*

I had absolutely no sort of political culture; I didn't grow up with any philosophical, intellectual, or religious influence, and everything I said about culture being the container of all allowed us to be protected from all of that for a long time. It didn't concern or bother us, we didn't experience it. That said, as soon as there was a real politicization, Marxism was the model of thought. We were impregnated by it. I think we went into it, myself included, much more savagely, more absolutely than we thought. It was still a very forceful remainder of a world of thought that was of great quality: that of having an answer for everything. What I liked about Marxism was that it was the thought that was able to say something essential, about goals, about the being of things, but which at the same time preserved in detail a certain enigma of the knowledge of processes. I am ashamed to admit it, but I really liked a certain kind of extremely dogmatic Marxist-Leninist literature, which we both read and published, because it contained the idea of a knowledge of ends and of our identity. I liked the idea that in no matter what speech there was this experience of struggle against the enemy, of a possible critical return, and of the analysis of a process. That's related to what I was saying earlier about the walker:

this idea of not wanting the landscape to be revealed at once, deferring until later and preferring to know how one moves towards an image or a landscape. Again as always it's this story of the tracking shot in *Kapo*: how do we approach an image? I imagined finding that theme again, even on the totally parched terrain of a quasi-tetralogical theory, which is a sort of crazy dialectic of its body, where one includes non-mastery in the process of mastery, and that gave me a kind of intellectual hard-on. I admired those who were capable of creating balance sheets, critiques, or auto-critiques. I found them so serious, pathetic, and derisory that I thought: one day we're going to make comedies about them. Unfortunately that day never arrived, except perhaps with Nani Moretti. There was a kind of absolutely sinister humor in the way of thinking the contradiction in itself, and to think it in such a rhetorical, precise, and minute way that finally the suspended part became more important than the believing part, the dogma or the holy scripture. Put differently: God wrote straight with crooked lines. All that never challenged the ultimate ends, but it gave us the *jouissance* of contradiction that has become almost erotic. Remember how in our essay that broke with the preceding line of *Cahiers*[1] I made an allusion to the Middle Ages by saying that the people must have quibbled over the *disputatio*. It was only our ignorance of history that made us believe we were inventing something. It's a sacred tradition that the people know a lot about. The eschatological part of Marxism, that is to say, the brighter tomorrows, and the liberation of humanity, I never believed it, not because I weighed the pros and cons, or because I thought humanity was bad, but simply because it never interested me. That became clear to me along the way, a total lack of imagination—which explains this mix of too serious and too careless—that I only believe in the phenomenological springing forth of things, and that's enough for me: after the rain comes the sun, after the sun comes the rain. Maybe it's a kind of stoicism, but already as a child, when at catechism we were taught about Paradise, I was revolted that someone could have recourse to such infantile fables when it was obvious that the eventual dignity of the human essence wasn't of that order. It was about doing good without expecting something in return. It was already an old revolt against the idea of bargaining between the concrete life, *hic et nunc*, and a promise that never interested me. What saved me from religion is that the other world is this world, and not the one that people tell you to dream about or desire, the "back worlds" that Nietzsche, who didn't believe in it either, spoke about, the "better worlds" or the brighter tomorrows, paradise on earth. That always seemed pathetic to me, a kind of shameful idea. It's the result of feeling as if I had been rescued *in extremis* in this very world, that this world exists and is correct. You have to present yourself well, without losing too many feathers, but this world is *already* the other world. If the stories of promises having to be realized down here or elsewhere never really interested me, I was willing to share this pleasure of processes with others, that of being there and of seeing how to think the real. That has nothing to do with Marxist philosophy, because I'm not a philosopher at all.

Something else that I liked about Marxism was its sense of history. I was always passionate for Marxism's ability to maintain an absolutely tragic and living sense of history: that of my own history, what it lacked: the history of France, of this contention never elucidated with France. Marxism had this air of romanticism that I liked.

You were confronted with Marxism at the same time that Cahiers *imposed it upon itself.*

When I look back with some coldness on my political past, I find that it makes sense based on the rest of my life. I'm not very proud of it, because at a certain moment carelessness and frivolity went a little too far. In the end I can clearly see the subjective reasons for it, but it has to be said that those at *Cahiers* were politicized collectively. It's more the defeat and disaster of a group, and before taking on my part in this disaster, I would say that collectively, one by one, we had to be unwell in order to need to stick to the group, to accompany it and to accompany oneself along the driveway towards the garage. Because obviously that's what it was: how could one believe in it? I never believed that it could create something, and I even hoped that it would create nothing. Can you imagine if our general line had succeeded? It was horrifying! For me it wasn't about a lucidity, but a true duplicity, a totally un-critical adherence to everything that was political—Yes to China, No to the USSR, No to the Communist Party—provided above all that it doesn't actually happen! I see in this the transition to the illness of something which was present at *Cahiers*, something positive in the beginning, but not so great later on. I would say that communism, like cinema, is the promise of a counter-society, a counter-society within society, which believes itself to be superior, which holds society in contempt, which denies society and thinks of itself as the carrier of what society doesn't recognize or fights against, with this idea that one day, later on, always later, we will see what we will see. All the same, this counter-society has the advantage of being a society. Thus for me, by choosing *Cahiers*, by assuming this manner of being a cinephile, in the will of being a part of this history (what the journal had just brilliantly represented: the New Wave), there was for me the will to be a part of a counter-society that would have all the benefits of a society, with its friendships, its passions, and its ruptures. In any case I had to make that wager on what cinema and communism shared. To transcend the nationalities and make a promise: cinema promised access to an undifferentiated world, that of humanity, all of humanity, while communism promised a gradual liberation from the human species. In waiting, a rather devoted, courageous, and disinterested counter-society was ready for anything, including the lie, even in the name of some obligatory truth. Again we come back to this history of the world and of society: when I speak about the world, there's something in me that opens up (as understood by Heidegger and Merleau-Ponty); when I speak of society, this same thing closes. Cinema is not of the realm of society, and neither is communism. The two, which make the history of a century, in a terrible way have that in common, and Marxism was its disciplinary tool. For someone who loves ideas and who has the taste for systems, it was pretty exciting in its everyday form of a dialectical exercise, like in Godard and Gorin's *Luttes en Italie*. There was something cold, but not without grandeur, in this kind of Jansenism of the contradiction having become its own body. This obviously happens a lot with Straub and Godard, but I remember having a strong sense that the Straubs called upon the types of political power of which they would be the first victims. They didn't seem to care, out of a sort of masochism that, as always, plays a positive role in *jouissance*. This came from the fact that it was possible to see the dialectic of nature and humanity happening before our eyes, this sort of dream that we never wanted to follow as much as we did with directors precisely like Straub and Godard. What they had in common as artists was being inspired by materialism, and stumbling upon a miracle. The filmmakers who counted for us at the time, and who remain important (here I will add Robert Kramer), were tapped into this, in my opinion, dangerous madness, because it's obviously dangerous to conceive of processes uniquely in themselves. This brings us very close to science, as with Godard, where suddenly there is no longer any difference between man and woman, or one cell and another. We all had this (not particularly brilliant) masochistic sentiment, nourished by the fantasy of breaking art's neck by moving closer to science or mysticism. Yes, to snap whatever artistic will we had inside us, or whatever was left of it. It's a pretty tough balance sheet, but I don't think any of us had the artistic desire, or a strong enough drive, to go through it and eventually come out. We preferred grimly falling into something sacrificial, which would lead us to disappear as a collective and as individuals, rather than being caught red-handed for not being the important creators like those who came before us—I have to say that the past masters kind of crushed us.

This whole story resembles a Tavianien scenario. It's not particularly courageous. It's not exactly the baroque choice of China that's in question, but I regret it because we let it turn into fascism pure and simple: the great proletarian Cultural Revolution. What's a shame is that it precludes our moralizing to others. To be honest with myself, I will never forget to what extent my neurotic interests and the temporary weaknesses of my ego sometimes took over, as if I had abused what I had said about my strange position, in relation to the cinema, the world, the other. At any given moment the price to pay becomes heavy. I paid it by being a part of *Cahiers*, and then… From there it's not difficult to comprehend on a much larger scale how intelligent people, intellectuals of the highest rank, preferred their own rather masochistic interests of *jouissance* to the exercising of a modicum of good sense. I think of my politicization as having been frivolous, but it was unavoidable that it should come to me in this form. I was so marginal that to be part of a gang of sublime marginals posed absolutely no problem for me. It gave me more pleasure than reconciling myself with my time. And as a traveler, I dreamt of China. I literally dreamt about it: I saw myself in a plane on the way to China and my heart was beating. When I went there for the first time in 1980, I truly had the absurd yet genuine feeling of being the only one at *Cahiers* to go and apologize, as if my arrival meant "I'm sorry."

During this period in the 1970s the "we" took precedence in your speech and writing, a slightly sacrificial "we." It wasn't really your style.

It was at the same time something horrifying, a superego, and a kind of worthless gratification mixed together. If I hadn't had someone with me whom I could talk to every day, I wouldn't have lasted a week, and this someone was you. By then I was already quite a talker; having no one to talk to would have sunk me. I'm not very good at calculating, and I manipulate rather poorly, so the only power left to me is talking, and I always talk too much. Today I have the benefits of this "too much," but I still say too much without ever worrying about the effects. I learned by doing first, and thinking later. During that time we were creating one issue after another and making the adjustments. For five years I did nothing but adjust, not too fast or there would have been a short-circuit, and not too slow because we would have stalled. It's always the same process: at what speed does one get better? Even if I came out of it a little anemic, this speed was right. Each new issue of *Cahiers* liberated something, and little by little the words came back: "art," "body," "fascination." Then our itinerary itself became interesting again. It was thus by being the one who expects a certain truth from progression that, without realizing it, I became a journalist. So I tried to purge myself of the pure administration of cinema, without regret.

CHAPTER 8

Experience: From *Cahiers du cinéma* to *Libération*

Do you have a sort of ideal of fraternity? Basically, at Cahiers *first and then* Libération, *a much wilder environment, you always searched for the same type of relationship with those around you.*

Yes, I reproduced it at *Libé* a little more successfully, and doubtlessly with more authority. Even if it awoke in me a little late, I always had this desire or ideal to be part of a group of egos or strong and different personalities, bound by the same belief or by the fact of having the same enemies. In this desire there is something of the dream of a communist counter-society: birds of a feather... But, being a crazy individualist, it was equally necessary that everyone was absolutely singular in their lives, including their private lives. What bound us together at *Cahiers* was less friendship and more a belief. I chased after this image that never came, so at some point I found myself more important than it. To keep the boat from sinking I became the tiller-man, with all the problems that brings. I did it for myself, to save my own skin. But saving my skin meant saving *Cahiers*. In leaving *Cahiers* at 35 years old I experienced the most important crisis of my life, with a very strong sense of having wasted my life, of not existing, or of having completely forgotten to live by keeping myself safe in a middle ground. You remember, there were two moments in my life where I was ashamed to belong to something idiotic. The first was when Louis Marcorelles (whom I never liked and who never liked me) didn't deign to mention our names in his article for *Le Monde* on the thirtieth anniversary of *Cahiers*. I thought that my name would never appear in *Le Monde*, that newspaper which is all the same a civil state, and that brought back my illegitimate birth, being a bastard...The second was the Berri Affair last year, concerning *Uranus*.[1] I have to say that the idea of "one for all and all for one" took a serious blow. I hoped that, just like in the movies, friends would come out from everywhere, with everything stopping, and saying, "What the hell is goin' on here? We're gonna pummel the guy that's hassling our friend." It wasn't all that serious in itself, but no one came out. Today, if I wasn't sick, I would have definitely written them off, at the risk of finding myself even more isolated. Maybe I'm strong enough to be alone. One day, we understand that each saves his own skin; it's the truth of subjects. This idealization, based on the model of *The Three Musketeers*, is what is political in me. Political in the sense that it is a dream of an alliance among different people. After '68, the rights of the individual began to exist in a forceful way, and the ideal didn't consist in allying oneself with people who resembled one too much, but in learning how to make more refined alliances on more transversal ideals. That was the grandeur of the 1970s; whether it was in the movement of ideas or of mores, it was a slightly bitter grandeur that ended up smashing against its limits.

Could we come back to this point when Cahiers du cinéma *had to be saved? Now that you have some distance from it, how do you analyze that period?*

I took over *Cahiers* in 1973–1974, which was the true turning point of the decade: the oil crisis, the end of the "glorious thirty years" (*trente glorieuses*), the advertising boom, the Khmer Rouge entering Phnom Penh, the end of the Vietnam War, Solzhenitsyn, the death of Pasolini, Ferreri's *Last Woman*, Godard's *Numéro deux*, Eustache's *La Maman et la putain* ... We could clearly see that it was harder and harder for some to advance in experimentation: the avant-garde gaiety was over. This dispossession wasn't only mine or that of *Cahiers*. In relation to today, some rather grandiose things retain a lot of bitterness and nerve, so that we will soon be better able to perceive this moment in a different and more sympathetic way. The balance sheet of these *Cahiers* years isn't extraordinary. I thought that by being at *Cahiers*, we would be the heirs of a celebrated generation and that we ourselves would become exalted. In fact in singularizing ourselves we made a lot of mistakes. We almost sunk the ship. Then we courageously reset it afloat and the journal survived. The paradox is that everything I failed at at *Cahiers*, I was successful with at *Libération*, which was thus the perfect opposite of this kind of laborious work. But I had to go through a sort of hazing at *Cahiers* to realize suddenly that... It's like a nightmare, a bad dream which dissipates, and you wonder why the cloud has passed. I quickly realized that it was easier to write "I" at *Libération*, and above all that I had an enormous backlog of writing. All that I should have written in the previous ten years finally came out. I should also say that the film department that I managed to create was 80% homosexual, which made a huge difference...

The prude Cahiers...

Yes, disembodied. There was a sort of coming out. There was an extraordinary period at *Libération*; everything was done in an indescribable mess, but I could get my ideas across, the idea I had of cinematic treatment. It's a good memory for everyone and it lasted a few years. But there was no longer this fraternity ideal; it was way too uncontrollable because the people were really very peculiar.

Could we say that their good fortune was due to the fact that they barely had a history?

Some of them, those who were just starting, had no history.

There wasn't any mourning, contrary to Cahiers.

Right, there was no mourning yet, but a beautiful vitality. It was a lively place for people like Michel Cressole, Hélène Hazera, or Guy Hocqenghem, who fearlessly carried on a work of cultural agitation, furiously and provocatively. The newspaper was theirs by right. I added to that a serious cinephilia, but written less seriously.

So overall you took the word "liberation" literally.

Yes, it's *my* liberation. As in screenplays for kids' movies, everything happens very quickly. I wasn't well at all, and fifteen days later everything was fine. The essential thing is that it contributed towards the unity of all the rest of the Parisian cinephiles, with those thrilled to see someone continuing to represent them in their newspaper. That was a good period, five or six years, where I worked a lot more than at *Cahiers*, because at *Cahiers* we didn't do a lot, *one was worked*—which is to say, I didn't do much. At *Libération*, in addition to the timing, I learned to love the constraints of the present: a perfect newspaper has no sense, it is irregular by nature, but with the promise of being better the next day. I still believe in this ideal of the irregularity of life, in a sort of meteorology linked to the processes: the sun and the clouds; as with Renoir, one waits, in the small or large frames, but one waits nonetheless. That's why I was surprised to feel finally at ease at a newspaper; I discovered it with stupefaction, because I never thought I would have anything to do with journalism. But today I think that it was another facet of this same exigency of the walker, that of someone who only counts on himself, who only has his body: as long as no one touches his body, and as long as no one beats him, he goes where he wants, because it's absolute *jouissance* to go where one wants. I remember a stay in Cuba where having coffee with some kid took the whole afternoon; you had to use cunning, ditch a few cops, and pretend not to know each other. No need for the exhaustive evidence of Castro imprisoning and torturing people, since having a coffee with a Cuban was almost impossible. But for me there is no liberty more basic than this: to go where you want, the café of your choice, without letting yourself be imposed upon by anything whatsoever. Sometimes I get trapped inside my darkest neurosis; nevertheless that freedom is sacred. So, if there had been a little more respect for essential freedoms, if the communists hadn't been part of those who seek the sense in life instead of life itself, they would have refused this ridiculousness immediately, in the name of the very simple argument that a country where you can't have coffee with whomever you want is not free, and it's not worth the trouble of defending.

There is one essential thing that I have to say because it's worth everything and protected me my entire life from the big disasters, one thing allowed me to swim like Blanchot's *Thomas the Obscure*, never in the middle of the swimming pool but… It's a feeling of protection that I had very early on, in the same way that every experience belongs to the person who lived it. Whether this experience is worthless or passionate, no one will take it away; it is inalienable. Even when sometimes I did nothing of interest, this feeling never left me: I didn't have the same experience as others at the same time. The essential thing is to preserve the richness of this experience, not to devalue it; it is our only asset, and if we are in it deeply, it will spare us of want, jealousy, resentment, fascism, all the things that make life impossible for so many. I am impervious to envy; it is perhaps my sanctity. The only thing which interests me is to understand how the other gets along, to know his parameters, what he fights with, what he aims for, and what that produces. Its something that the two of us have in common, it's the way in which we resemble each other: this questioning of what the motor force of the individual or subject is. This sort of theoretical gossip is extremely interesting to me. Because the strength of cinema is what gives us this incredible access to other experiences besides our own, which allows us to share, if only for a couple of seconds, something very different. And what we have in common is precisely these few seconds. I'm very grateful to cinema for this because it's an idea I've had since childhood: what I'm doing right now, I'm the only one who is doing it, who sees it and who's conscious of it. And if Christian ideology needs to be struggled against, it's because it removes this minimal protection that you have only what you experience, and that you are the only one who experiences it. The history of the century, with all its horrors, is also the history of those who haven't seen, who haven't trusted what they saw, or heard, and that was paid for with millions of dead. That's insufficient, that doesn't prevent being mistaken or deluded, but it's good to go back to the argument of a sorrowful Godard when, in *Histoire(s) du Cinéma*, he asks: can we not watch one last time what the people weren't able to or didn't want to see, and what resulted from their refusal to see? This good side of selfishness brings out a classical materialism. The other half is religious and I also have a foot in this side: the people need intercessors, smugglers, priests, knowing that there might be a few bastards among them. At some point, because of our powerlessness to judge our own *jouissance*, we need someone else to do it for us.

Wouldn't you have changed from the status of a failed priest at Cahiers *to that of the smuggler of today, that is to say, someone who allows others to ally themselves to an historical experience, to cinephilia, to recognize oneself there, to find what they need there?*

I've become a bit of a guru at the end of my life, like someone we go to see in secret to get fixed up. Obviously I must have desired this status, worked towards it, but it only satisfied one part of me, that of the clandestine walker. On the other hand it bullied the public recognition side. In general, the people who come to acknowledge me do so in secret. This is what made me so upset last year, and in fact you were upset that I was so upset. These people who come to you say to you under a secret seal (oath) that they have chosen you as a master, they admire you or they find you to be essential, all of which is pleasurable, but the day you need them they're nowhere to be found. It's the price to pay, and I paid out of my own pocket. I represent, myself more than my words or what I write, a certain pure relationship to cinema, a certain claim, and it's extremely important to some people, but I don't have the right to satisfy myself by being the director of their conscience; it's a form of bargaining in which I don't get back much.

With you I often had the same feeling that I had at a certain period with Godard, that of being with a friend whom I admire, whom I like listening to, but in whom I don't really know how to follow, or understand in my own way, the intellectual process. There is in effect this form of saintliness, which is seductive and attractive, but which I also sense brings out an experience that is not completely shared.

I now really understand what Godard was saying at the time. For us, that kept the idea intact that *it didn't happen.*

And we were pretty glad that It didn't happen.

Yeah, we were content that "it wasn't happening," but I don't measure at all to what extent it didn't happen. Godard put us on the path. Today, I'm able to reproduce these intellectual procedures or the discourse close to his—in the end, close to the Godard of that period, since I don't really know where he is now. Without a doubt, there is in the *jouissance* of someone like him a part that is not communicable.

In talking about Godard, Jacques Rancière used the term *passeur*. The *passeur* is he who reserves the *jouissance* for himself up to the last word. There is thus a form of competition in which to be the last one is to be more and more grand. Godard is perhaps the last great filmmaker, myself perhaps the last critic to which that applies… This pride which consists of wanting to represent a terminal state or a legendary memory is difficult to present socially; there must be a sort of contradiction there, a double bind, which we put people in, and which would effectively explain that they are absolutely incapable of …

Because we have to give them time to have their own experience, which they can be conscious and proud of. Since that takes an absurd amount of time, it's easier to defer it onto another.

I wonder if this absurd amount of time is not just the normal time. We were all so twisted, we shouted in vain that the ideology of communication accelerates everything and that it's horrifying, but we didn't really internalize it. Everything that is transmission belongs to that sphere: first we were impregnated with a music, then a language, then a voice, and then comes the manner of finding the arguments and one says: I finally understand, but in fact I always understood.

And that could take an entire lifetime.

In spite of ourselves we are victims of this ideology of communication, which wants us to sum ourselves up within a form. It's a bit like psychoanalysis: we always knew but we didn't have access to what we understood, we always know everything there is to know, but we can't access this knowledge. What grants access to that knowledge is simply life. For me this is always how it happened: later on I had the feeling of understanding things which weren't so difficult, although it took a long time and I had to very willfully try to understand them. It was when I stopped reading Lacan that what I read in his books seemed more comprehensible to me. I didn't have official approval, but the Lacan I read serves me, and it doesn't matter at all to me if it isn't orthodox. I can see myself in a big hotel in Belgrade, the "Serbia," in the middle of winter, reading *Écrits* and not understanding anything, convinced that I absolutely had to catch up with those at *Cahiers* who had read it. I was pretty worthless, I had barely read Freud, and I can see myself reading down line by line with a card in order to not go too fast. It took twenty years to understand that it wasn't so magical. I regret not having done philosophy, because with Merleau-Ponty and Heidegger I would have had a foundation. I wanted to be taken care of by the cinema, to be saved from society and put into the world through very complicated procedures, to end up representing all of that in the eyes of others. What happened to me is certainly very logical; in the meantime cinema has become this totally ambiguous thing: weaker and weaker in reality and at the same time stronger and stronger in a culture's symbolic cache. In some way I benefit from this cache, not so much as an individual, because my life is completely banal, but through a sort of sanctification of the film geek.

CHAPTER 9

Cinema and Television: Departure and Return

It seems to me that cinema draws upon the metaphor of the hourglass, the flowing of time, what has already past and what's still to live. Basically cinema had a century to tell stories, and to get on board the century with its own history. For reasons difficult to explain you get the impression of a countdown, and we don't know if there is still a lot of sand left. At the point where you are today, touching the dividends of this cache that you speak about, doesn't the state of cinema incite in you the desire to walk in a new direction?

With what you just said I can make the link with this story of television. When I took over at *Cahiers* we went to see Daniel Sibony, Paul Virilio, Pierre Legendre, and Jean-Louis Schefer, thinkers who were mysterious and more complicated than we were, and I asked Louis Skorecki to write about television and Jean-Paul Fargier about video; I was thus already something of a journalist and not at all satisfied being confined to pure cinephilia. At *Libération*, there was this sea snake to wrangle, a veritable "image department," because it has to be said that during the 1980s the word "image" was everywhere, positive, happy, and the carrier of meaning. It was about continuing what was started at *Cahiers*, because I didn't want to return to the whir of industry where nothing of importance is ever born. On this point I haven't changed much, even if I've made peace with it. I was looking for where this might come from, from where it could get its new impetus. Television, for instance. The ideal of an "image department" implied that we stop giving cinema a cultural privilege which disgusted us—when I was young I expected too much from culture not to be disgusted by the cultural. That consisted of taking television seriously: watching it, saying good things about it when it was called for, keeping informed about the evolution of video, and being interested in all images. It would take us many pages to say that some commercial or some film was an event, through the improvised hierarchy of the daily news. It's an idea I renounced when I stopped working on cinema at *Libération*, no longer believing in its happy ecumenism. Today it's about putting the cinema, and only the cinema, back into a history that will no longer be synchronic, but rather diachronic: from which came the idea of creating *Trafic*. Ever since History disappeared, the concern about history has returned: the questions of genealogy and origins are again objectively asked. It's true that today the history of cinema seems very passionate to me, but I would prefer to classify it with Lascaux and Nadar rather than with Bernard Dufour and Averty. They are other alliances, because cinema has to be coupled with something else to function well: it's still this idea of cinema as an impure art. Moreover, I am not even sure what this idea of an impure art means for Bazin, but I know what it means for me: the truth of cinema is recording; moving away from it is moving away from cinema. Except that what is recorded can have quite a history. We shouldn't be afraid of putting this art of recording in relation to an even older history of the image in Western societies, of using theology. I don't expect anything from a cinema that would find nourishment in itself; the best case scenario of this are the films of Alain Corneau, and that's not sufficient. Perhaps at *Libération* I was an arrogant and luxurious character, writing with total freedom; I could have had the humility to continue until my essays caused problems, but I sensed that I began to represent for people a sort of symbolic and vigilant presence, and it was out of the question to become some sort of a "Mr. Cinema."

Did you ever think in terms of equivalence: perhaps similar to Hollywood during the studio era, television could be understood as an industry wildly producing signs—and there would always be people to analyze and decode them—something the cinema, becoming precisely too cultural, was no longer able to assure?

We could have loved the cinema in the name of the avant-garde, from a place where one wouldn't owe anything to anyone. That's not exactly the script we followed, whether it was Jean-Claude Biette, Louis Skorecki, or myself. We chose the cinema with good reason, with its terrible commercial fate, always taking the side of the artist over the producer—the artist was always the hero of the story. And the beauty came precisely from the fact that the cinema would take its heterogeneous, impure materials and produce an unexpected beauty. I always liked the fact that cinema was made with all the things I had trouble controlling: money, the terrifying and vulgar demands of commerce, the desire for one another on a shoot, the stars and their caprices, the necessity of directing a team, of taming and seducing, the relationship with time, the obligation to plan, to make plans... All that makes a film, nothing but a film, from which it is possible to take for oneself such and such an element and to do with it as one pleases. It's therefore a love of cinema in so far as it's about an impure practice, on the basis of a great mistrust towards the other arts, condemned to a certain purity, as a result of the rarefaction of a certain vulgarity of the demand and response of the audience.

Did I believe that television offered the same "scenario," but just bigger and more bloated? Probably. What's certain is that television has nothing to do with impurity, but situates itself in the openly unconscious interference of society. There isn't enough love in it for us to even have the perverse desire of reading it, or analyzing its signs as with cinema, which invites us to do so. That's why I think that at the time we were still real semiologists, or at least influenced by semiology. There were certain rather priggish after-effects of Barthes' work on us as well: images, being signs, gave us all the right to avoid them, to *detourn* them, without much concern since a sign wasn't anything more than a little piece of code. At the time, the fact that television produced large amounts of signs and rhetoric didn't bother us. From there, to consider that television became the equivalent of cinema, under the pretext that it would fulfill the same functions at a mass level, is what many must have hoped for, at the risk of diminishing their aesthetic tastes and to accept going from the absolute refinement of Howard Hawks' *mise-en-scène* to the simplified and rather pale telefilm. We risked renouncing, in the name of a certain masochism, what ended up being our asset. In this relationship with television, the exercise consisted in wanting to control not the various beauties, but the truths, or rather the right positions in relation to barely elaborated, very dogmatic, and trivial material. When I arrived at *Libération*, I remember that Michel Cressole and Guy Hocquenghem had this terrific attitude which consisted of watching everything, without any kind of system, with only one criterion: either we like it or we don't, we take it or leave it, we detest such and such announcer and we take pot shots at him. It wasn't about any deep truth, the only truth being that television calls for target practice. That had the advantage of putting television back in its place as an object, worthy of interest, by avoiding contempt and adoration, two complicit attitudes that offer nothing. Following them Skorecki tried to apply to television series what he had already done with cinema at *Cahiers*. Paradoxically writing just and true things about a TV series, while even those who watched and loved them, without, however, valorizing them, were not expecting anyone to write about them, and heinously making use of them as a war machine against the noble bourgeois culture: it's something I'm able to understand, although this project comes late, and transforms whoever practices it into an irritating misanthrope.

No matter what, I would have stopped writing about television. What's strange is that on the one hand I'm stronger than it, and on the other it's much stronger than I am, and these two forces are heterogeneous. It's enough to watch any television program to be in a position to bring back the Western metaphysic, establishing that television never *worked*. But its strength resides in the fact that those who make it have impunity and can tolerate some impoverished critic's protests. They have the impunity of the mafia, to such an extent that you decide it's impossible to win this war, the war Godard was fighting when he said that television had to be taken as our collective destiny, or as the only public space that remains, even if it's trashed, and all we can do is begin to work with that public space. Today we should leave this approach to the sociologists and statisticians, to the "Mr. Homais" of the world. I was forced to take on the fact that I could no longer look anywhere else but the cinema for the rest of this political history of impurity, that which makes us citizens. I thought that cinema addressed itself to subjects, or it helped in constituting subjects, by a sort of very slow collective psychoanalysis, and that in the best case scenario, television would contribute to the reinforcement of the citizen, which is a completely different problem, calling upon different aesthetic questions.

To sum up, I didn't wait for what followed from cinema in cinema, except at the periphery: I didn't pay much attention to the underground or video, conscious that great things could happen there but without any dialectical link with the cinema, or else via a few individual experiences. As for new images, about which we have heard so much for the last ten years, I have again become a Marxist: there is something called the market, and it has to be ready to welcome true and great new contributions, in terms of images and sounds, which can't be reduced to the state of appliances and the rivalry between Sony and Phillips. That takes place at a purely economic level; there is a corporate battle with the possibilities of new images of which no one sees the ludic after-effects, precisely in the interior of this public space, and which would again be able to amaze the public like it did almost a hundred years ago with the arrival of the train at La Ciotat. We don't see the desire for a new *Train en gare de La Ciotat* anywhere. Some say arrogantly that cinema is very beautiful with its old moons, and its extravagances, but in five years people will have giant interactive screens. It's possible, except that the timing of the event, which in my opinion is very slow, has to be respected. Like Bazin I think that the desire or need for the cinema must have been overwhelming, like a forest fire, and that was unique in the history of art. I struggled against this idea a lot, because I wanted cinema to inscribe itself in the linear unfolding of the world, after photography and before television or video. It was a comfortable thought that allowed for a continuation. Well, mistaken once again, as always when one thinks in linear terms. In fact there is a spiral, and the question is not asked on the side of technique, but on the side of a mass desire to again be amazed by the visual and the aural. The only time I ever had that feeling was watching Zbigniew Rybczinski's *Quatrième dimension* on Canal+ , and I thought that this videaste had the technical means to realize an absolutely profound and basic human fantasy, and that left me completely flabbergasted. I went to the geode[1] to be amazed; I came back disappointed. It's possible that we are in a sort of interminable turning, which hinders existing technology from being able to adapt itself to the market, and that there is a blockage due to the fact of economic war. If Warner Bros. hadn't behaved so poorly in 1928, the talkie might have waited a few more years because of this sort of *omerta*. The beauty of cinema is that it is an art where Garrel made the same gestures as Griffith; there's a sort of anthropological memory of gestures, like Eisenstein unrolling a bit of film in his hand to look at it. In the face of this mass desire which never ceases to appear, one participates in the development of the rhetoric of individuals and individualism that takes place in commercials, and which is still in the process of affirming its power. The aesthetic subject is thus the individual, he who must be reformed, and the commercial is the instrument of this reforming.

Is this not also the principal role of television?

It reforms the presence of the individual at the interior of collective rituals, which are in fact the collective rituals of shopping, villages, and nations: the horror! The two advance at the same time, advertising being the aesthetic matrix, television the place of mass application. It's either horror or the future, but either way it's a true debate.

Are you saying that there is little chance for cinema to find its fortune again?

I don't see how cinema can represent anything other than a red line or a contestation.

Or a "that took place."

That took place, yes: a critique. What's extraordinary is for us the train in the La Ciotat station still keeps arriving, a century later. It's still possible to put oneself in the position of the frightened spectator, which means that there is something in cinema that is of the past but not past.

Out of which comes Lumière's famous line: cinema, an invention without a future.

It is an art of the present which has a way of passing. Its future is its past, which is the photograph, and maybe there is a kind of odd circle or involution: everything is possible. What I don't believe at all is that when something seems to disappear it is immediately replaced by something else.

CHAPTER 10

The Two Cinemas

We can ask the question again transversally: throughout the century were true filmmakers only those who resisted cinema's natural tendency to become an industrial art? Basically, wouldn't cinema itself be an exception within the entertainment industry, and would its history, from the point of view of a journal like Cahiers du cinéma, *concern only the filmmakers who defended a certain idea of cinema against the cinema itself, knowing that it faced an industry that would move it away from this art of recording invented by the Lumière Brothers?*

I've thought for a long time that there are two kinds of cinema: one kind represents 80% of cinema, the other barely 20%. One part of cinema was the recording pure and simple of what people wanted to see, no matter what the cost, on the condition that the image was clear. Right from the start the audience wanted to see the Passion of Christ via cinema.

Already the son et lumière *that doesn't announce itself as such.*

Yes, pious films which came from Sulpician painting, or in reference to certain poses transmitted by a religious culture. One part of the audience was totally indifferent to the fact that this machine could serve something other than filming the Tsars. As a result Lumière had this flash of genius to send cameramen all over the place, to film Delhi street scenes as well as the Romanov royalty; everything that the audience wanted to see, by simple adherence and fascination, pure and sincere—the kings, queens, and exotic landscapes—passed through cinema. For example, in Italy there was a whole production in the teens and 1920s about strong men and the phenomenon of the carnival, it was enough to just film someone doing tricks, films without stories; we wanted to see monsters. A list should be made of what people wanted to see independent of mediation, that is to say, of its foundation.

It's this part of cinema from which television in a certain way picked up the torch.

Absolutely. And then there is the complex phenomenon of stars, of which there are two kinds: those who are the creation of cinema (the most pure being Garbo, who didn't exist outside of cinema, and the fact that she stopped so early is a sign that perhaps it was a limited period of time), and those who were made by the circus, cabaret, singing, or opera. A part of cinema that we neither watched nor studied depends on the more or less technically correct recording of a performance; it is this popular culture that has no perception of the machine: it doesn't matter if it's a drawing, a painting, or a photograph that moves. It's what popular culture always has as a base, a call to mythology, because mythology is independent of foundation; it's a black box, not a process. Every society has images, or scenes, which it wants to see no matter what the cost. It should be known that in India ticket sales are dropping slightly, even though it holds the most movie theaters in the world; they even resemble temples—and, in the poorest villages, they show videos in every little greasy spoon. It's the same all throughout Asia: the loss of definition and size of the image is unfathomable. This basically renders Bazin correct: there are pious, social images that we'll see under any conditions: this relativizes the argument of those who deify the movie theater, and the so-called "encounter with the people." Yes, there must have been at another time an osmosis between the people and the movie theater, but I think that the need for images in a society is something much more brutal. This isn't about criticism, it's a mythological function of society that has to be used or studied such as it is. Obviously we can always say that at one time there was Chaplin, the actor and the director. If one is to be nostalgic, it should be for that moment in cinema: Chaplin, Keaton, the American burlesque, with this simultaneous double creation where the actor created the social myth at the same time as the machine for showing it. That didn't last beyond the talkie. Being generous, 20% of cinema was interesting, where what counted was less what one filmed than the recording apparatus: the interest was displaced onto the machine, on to the camera itself and the effects it induced, on the possibilities of editing, and on movement. It's the only part of cinema whose history we can retrace, that we can follow, from Lumière through the present, passing by Dziga Vertov. At a certain moment in cinema it was the procedure of recording that became in itself fascinating or intriguing, loveable or uncomfortable for some. The rest is about the recording of things already won, already of the majority, already dominant. Through my own history, I could only have a relationship to this cinema where you are taken by the hand by someone with a name, the author, and who says to you: Here it is, this is how I look at the world, this is how I find myself in it, come with me and you'll have a coherent vision of it.

It's another way of defining what we called the "politique des auteurs."

I forgot to say one thing which is in some way the missing link between the tracking shot in *Kapo* and what we were just talking about: the problem, after this mix of desire and terror in relation to the image, is to get close to the image and to enter inside it. The cinephilic fantasy in the final analysis is that of *Sherlock Junior* or *Les Carabiniers*: to enter inside, not like a little imbecile on whom the screen falls, and not like a hero either (*à la* Keaton), but rather as if one were learning to swim in a different space. Swimming is *mise-en-scène*. It's in this sense that I spoke about the frame as the *sine qua non* condition of everything, camera movement or not, montage or not, details or not, close-ups or not, modulation or not, in the final analysis it's only about showing or not. The cinephile is the one who enters the real space of the movie theater which represents society and the imaginary space; it's false to think that there is only one line, or one frontier. Only the naïve think we swing all of a sudden into another space, as in *The Purple Rose of Cairo*. In fact, between these two spaces there exists a third, structured like a tennis court. When we truly look at this obsessional line many forms can be played there, the forms of admission and rejection, those of the net: at what point do we stay on this side of the net, at what point does the *mise-en-scène* take us by the hand and give us the right to step over the net or to make a passing shot?

When you fetishize the *mise-en-scène* like I do, you know that there's an intermediary zone, a limbo, which means that when watching a film we don't simply go from real life to dream life, like the somewhat naïve thinking of the surrealists, but there is an intermediary zone between the two. And all the *politique des auteurs* consisted of was testing this partner who is the auteur, the one who teaches us to play. That's why *Moonfleet* is the most beautiful cinephilic film, the positive version of *Night of the Hunter*: the little boy demands to have a father, he chooses him and insists that he act as his father, even though the other prefers to act otherwise, and he expects lessons on *mise-en-scène* from him, that is to say, lessons of topology, the lessons of recognizing the territory. One of Lang's most beautiful lines is when the little boy says, "The exercise was beneficial, sir." Little John Mohune decides that he is going to follow Jeremy Fox (Stewart Granger) exactly as I decided to follow Fritz Lang. The image of the auteur is a paternal image, but the father isn't there, and it's preferable that he isn't there too much so that the figure of the auteur can be fetishized. Never being really interested in the biographies of great directors, I preferred to think that when you follow an auteur in his way of locating himself in the world, you attain a certain quantum of truth, which isn't the same whether it's Hitchcock, Lang, or Bresson. That's what the *politique des auteurs* is for me. It poses itself in terms of acceptance or refusal: I can refuse to enter into a film, like, for example, the tracking shot in *Kapo*; I'm not someone who you take by the hand in just any old way. But if I'm angry at Potecorvo, it's precisely because someone has to take me by the hand, it's absolutely necessary that someone says to me, "I'm sorry but I saw this shot, I edited it before you and now I show it to you," for me to respond, "The way you showed it to me makes me want to see it, at my own risk, so that the film can tell me *my* story." All the same, in the twentieth century cinema invented one or two things that are of the order of Deleuzian concepts, pure concepts: the shot. Ultimately I don't know if we can say concept, so let's say the shot and the out of frame, that which, moreover, works at the same time (the shot can have the out of field as its motive force). Even though we were completely right to be interested in those ideas in the

1970s, we had a very formalist vision of them, because obviously it creates effects of sudden death, of beauty, of rupture; we read about the effects of Eisenstein, who was a rather hedonistic theorist, who maintained his *jouissance*. But with Tod Browning it's mind-blowing, a director who is the antithesis of Eisenstein and at least as great. Concerning the monstrosity and montage, it could be said that *Freaks* is a response to *Strike*. There are thus different ways of creating shots, in every sense of the term. We can't say that at *Cahiers* we didn't see the disappearance of shots coming. Today it's so deep into it …

… that one bathes in the visual and in the ideology of the visual.

Which for me is not the same as the image. It's Pavlovian. Sometimes figures emerge in the visual, for example in music videos, as nice surprises, but totally disconnected from the idea of the shot. I think that the change was prepared, the notion of the shot was dynamited, by modern cinema; there was even a sort of obstinacy. Now it's done and we don't have the same energy to describe in terms of formal violence what governs even the images that we watch today. It's what surprises me the most. With the Hitchcock effect, for example, there is no efficacy, there is the idea that *cinema can do it*: a true formal aggression that has totally disappeared. In the history of cinema there is only a small part of cinema that recounts and theorizes itself via film journals, by the simple fact that at a certain moment it's the process for approaching the real which is more intriguing or interesting than the thing figured, reproduced, or represented. But to come to this conclusion, we have to get rid of a vision which is paradoxically invasive and very shy and modest, from the 1970s, around this famous idea of the specificity of the cinema. Cinema had to have its specificity. I think this is somewhat similar with the new images: we are going to end up forgetting that there had been a great sublime promise a long time ago, and we forgot that it needed to be carried by a desire. It had to be filled in this interim where we are and where we risk remaining a long time. I tried to anticipate what was coming and I got tired. So in the end I accepted the idea that the cinema was or had been so extraordinary that we could have made a trimestral journal, for example, that it would incite writing more, and that in this way it would transmit the experiences of a few. Because I was tired of seeing nothing coming. We don't expect an amazement as unforgettable as what we had known. We don't expect anything unforgettable. We are even rather anxious about an eventual "Orwellian" becoming of great mass audio-visual ceremonies, giant telethons on a big screen. Yes, fascism… Are we stopping?

Notes

Preface to the French Edition

1 The original French title for the current translation.
2 "Lettre sur Rossellini," *Cahiers du cinéma*, 46, April 1955.

Chapter 1 The Tracking Shot in Kapo

1 Probably referring to the abridged version of George Sadoul's monumental *Histoire du cinéma mondiale*. The complete version ran to four volumes.
2 A term *Cahiers* critic Jean-Louis Comolli used about Eric Dolphy. The literal translation is *smugglers*, the idea being someone who confers or passes on a kind of forbidden knowledge. As will be seen, the term is used often with Daney, as he too becomes a kind of *passeur*. Daney also makes reference to Jacques Rancière's use of the term.
3 Henri Agel, film critic and author of, among other books, *Esthétique du cinéma* in the series *Que sais-Je?*
4 One of the rare female critics at *Cahiers du cinéma*.
5 A raid on 16 July 1942 which Vichy France used to show support for the Gestapo. Jews were rounded up voluntarily by the French authorities and deported to Drancy.
6 *Cinéfils* is a play on the word "cinephile," where *fils*, the French word for son, replacing *-phile*, renders a word along the lines of *cine-son*. In the documentary interview with Daney directed by Pierre-André Boutang and conducted by Régis Debray, the English translation of *cinéfils* is "film-buff kid." It's left here in the original French to retain the integrity that the phonetic similarity creates.
7 Université Sorbonne Nouvelle, Paris III.
8 The thirty years of economic productivity after the Second World War.

9 Robert Faurisson is a French revisionist historian who was fired from his university position for claiming that the Holocaust never occurred.

Chapter 2 Cine-biography

1 Located on rue Keller in the 11th arrondisement in Paris. [*Endnote in original*]
2 *Il deserto dei Tatari* by Dino Buzzati (Milan: Rizzoli, 1940). The book tells the story of a young officer dispatched to an area which he waits for over thirty years to defend against attack and thus acquire a modicum of glory. To his chagrin, no attack ever occurs.
3 A collection of pocket books.
4 L'enfant Ernesto is a character in the Straubs' short film *En rachâchant*, based on a children's story by Marguerite Duras. [*Endnote in original*]
5 Phonetic rendering of *La main qui étreint.*
6 Reference to the Octave Mannoni essay of the same name published in *Clefs pour l'imaginaire ou L'Autre Scène* (Paris: Seuil, 1985).
7 Film by Luis Buñuel from 1956.
8 A dictionary and encyclopedia in a single volume.
9 Afrique Occidentale Française and Afrique Equatoriale Française
10 Institut Géographique National.
11 Gilles Deleuze wrote a letter to Daney that serves as the introduction to *Ciné-journal.* The English translation can be found in *Negotiations* (New York: Columbia University Press, 1997), a collection of interviews and short works by Deleuze.
12 Hergé is the author of *Tintin* and Edgar Pierre Jacobs the author of *Blake and Mortimer.*
13 *La Rampe. Cahier critique 1970–1982* (Paris: Éditions Cahiers du cinema—Gallimard, 1983). [*Endnote in original*]
14 Reference to Cinéthiques collective film *Quand on aime la vie on va au cinéma*, the script of which appeared in *Cinéthique*, 17–18, 1974.
15 Phonetic rendering in French of Harry Baur.
16 Paul Touvier, a French war criminal accused of committing

crimes against humanity. Daney is referring to Touvier's provisional release granted in 1991. However, after Daney's death, Touvier was sentenced to life imprisonment and died in a prison hospital in 1996.

17 This phrase ended up as the title of Daney's posthumously published journal *L'exercice a été profitable, Monsieur* (Paris: P.O.L., 1993).

18 Refers to two Fritz Lang films from 1959, *Tiger of Bengal* (*Der Tiger von Eschnapur*) and *The Indian Tomb* (*Das indische Grabmal*). [*Endnote in original*]

19 Charles Péguy, French author of *Clio* (Paris: Gallimard, 1931).

20 "Sur Salador," in *Cahiers du cinema*, 222, July 1970. It was reprinted in *La Rampe*, p. 17. [*Endnote in original*]

21 *Histoire d'une revue*, by Antoine de Baecque (in two volumes) (Paris: Éditions Cahiers du cinema, 1991). [*Endnote in original*]

22 MacMahonians refers to those who frequented the MacMahon movie theater, which showed primarily American fare.

23 Louis Skorecki and Claude Dépêche.

24 "Frank and Jerry," on Frank Tashlin's *Who's Minding the Store?*, starring Jerry Lewis. [*Endnote in original*]

25 French legal term that in essence prevents a plaintiff from bringing a case before the court because too much time has elapsed or because the parties involved have reached a satisfactory agreement.

26 Mosfilm, the largest film and television production and post-production facility in Russia.

27 At the time the office of *Cahiers du cinéma* was located at 146 avenue des Champs-Elysées, and was under the direction of Jacques Doniol-Valcroze and Eric Rohmer. [*Endnote in original*]

28 États Généraux du Cinema was a political film group that formed around May 1968. The name is a reference to the États Généraux of 1789.

29 Silvina Boissonas, a rich patron of the arts around whom a group formed made up of Phillipe Garrel, Jackie Raynal, and others, who referred to themselves as the Zanzibar Group.

Chapter 3 Cinema and History

1 Refers to the project of the Revolution of 1789.
2 Albert Malet and Jules Isaac, French historians who co-authored *Histoire du France du XVI siècle à 1774*, among other pedagogical history course-books.
3 *Qualunquismo* is an Italian word derived from *Uomo Qualunque* or "everyman," whose meaning is political indifference or intolerance towards political parties.

Chapter 4 Cinephile in Transit

1 Journalist at *Libération.*
2 French national theater created in 1920 to bring theater to the general public.
3 Jean Vilar, French actor and director who revitalized the TNP as a forceful educational and creative influence in French life.

Chapter 6 Cinema Would be the Promise of the World

1 La Bibliothèque de la Pléiade: highly respected French collection of books that publishes works primarily of French authors.
2 Jean-Claude Biette (6 November 1942–10 June 2003): filmmaker, author, and co-founder of *Trafic.*
3 Mr. Homais refers to a character in Gustave Flaubert's *Madame Bovary*. Mr. Homais is characterized as pretentious, a pseudo-intellectual, and a coward.

Chapter 7 Cinema and Communism: In Defense of a Counter-society

1 Serge Daney and Serge Toubiana, "Les Cahiers aujourd'hui," *Cahiers du cinema*, 250, March 1974. [*Endnote in original*]

Chapter 8 Experience: *From Cahiers du cinéma* to *Libération*

1 See Serge Toubia's Preface above.

Chapter 9 Cinema and Television: Departure and Return

1 La Géode: a kind of amusement park with a cinema dome and a huge hemispheric screen.